Gems of Grace

A theologian of great repute has said that "there is no greater argument for the reality of authentic Christianity than a life transformed by the grace of God."

This is what makes *Gems of Grace* a book both significant and satisfying in today's inquiring world. It is siginificant because it illustrates the power of God's transforming grace: it is satisfying because it relates then to human situations as we really know them.

I warmly recommend this book.

STEPHEN F. OLFORD

Gems of Grace seems an extremely helpful and practical book which should meet the need of many readers. It is easily read, which is attractive to people in these days...

A. LINDSAY GLEGG

Infectious joy, ardent zeal, a sunny smile and a burdened heart... these are the characteristics of Bob Stokes and also of his writings. I always find inspiration from reading anything written by my friend...

FRANCIS W. DIXON

Gems *of* Grace

Bob Stokes

WALKING TOGETHER PRESS
ESTES PARK · JENTA MANGORO

© 2023 Walking Together Press

Published in 2023 by
Walking Together Press
Estes Park, Colorado USA
Jenta Mangoro, Jos, Plateau Nigeria
https://walkingtogether.press

ISBN: 978-1-961568-96-9

Published with permission

First published in 1972 by Mission Enterprises Melbourne
Text from the enlarged 1979 edition

Cover design by D. Thaine Norris
Typeset in Adobe Garamond Pro by D. Thaine Norris

1

Foreword

Bob Stokes, British born, a former missionary to India and the Fiji Islands and later an evangelist and convention speaker in Australia where his ministry was much blessed of God, was, in the providence of the Lord, led to visit the work of Trans World Radio in Monte Carlo in 1963.

We were immediately drawn to each other and shortly afterwards Bob was led to incorporate his ministry with that of T.W.R. For several years Bob continued in Australia under our sponsorship and opened an office in the city of Melbourne as our South Pacific Representative.

For the past four years he has shared a similar position as our Deputational Secretary in Britain. Bob has travelled extensively with his devoted wife, Cynthia, and has been much used of the Lord in creating interest in the world wide ministry of T.W.R. through his audio-visual presentation. His evangelistic and deeper life messages have resulted in deep dealings with God.

More recently We offered him a weekly programme over T.W.R's radio network from Monte Carlo and Bonaire. This morning feature is looked forward to by many listeners. May this selection of informal devotional radio talks, based on some telling human experiences of God's grace, be of great blessing to every reader.

Ralph Freed, D.D.
General Director
Trans World Radio
Monte Carlo
October 1972

Dedication

Dedicated to my devoted wife, Cynthia, whose charm of disposition, strength of character and loyalty of purpose have been a constant source of inspiration behind this human documentary of some of the Lord's dealings with us throughout thirty-five wonderful years together, for which we give Him all the glory.

October 8th 1972
(our wedding anniversary)

Acknowledgement

To all who have contributed towards the publication of this book by their Christian life and testimony, and to those who have painstakingly checked the proofs, the author gratefully acknowlegdes his indebtedness.

The publisher wishes to acknowledge Bob and Cynthia Stokes' children who have granted permission for this 2023 reprint, and have provided the back cover photograph from their personal collections.

Contents

1

A Young Man's Dilemma

*Ye shall seek Me, and find me, when
ye shall search for Me with all
your heart. (Jeremiah 29:13)*

It was a damp and misty night on November 5th. The pungent smell of burnt-out squibs and rockets added to the already thick atmosphere of an approaching winter. Flickering shadows cast by myriads of bonfires illuminating the ruddy faces of excited youngsters seemed to dance in ecstacy to the wild performance of stately roman candles, wobbly Catherine wheels and erratic jumping jackers. Shrieks of childish delight were mingled with the crash and boom of an artillery display costing only a few shillings. An occasional rocket burst into the starry heights leaving a train of glory in its wake.

All this was lost to a young man who was searching desperately for reality in a world which seemed to offer so little and yet promise so much. On that memorable November night

1

as he plodded through the murky haze of spent-out fireworks in the back streets of Strood, in Kent, there was one thought permanent in his mind; Was there a living God? If so, could He help a fellow in need?

His background was nothing out of the ordinary. Brought up in nominal Christian surroundings he had attended church services as long as he could remember. His parents had been good and kind and had even sacrificed to give him and his brothers a good education. Days of depression—the time was the 1930s—had adversely affected his father's business, so his scholarship to boarding school had been well worth while. Now he was on his own. This was his first venture into the unknown. He had just been apprenticed as a bank clerk. He was experiencing for the first time a sense of loneliness which is the inenviable lot of those who have never found the Saviour.

His mother was a simple-hearted Christian who had taught him to pray at her knees. He was deeply thankful for this. As a very young boy he had also learned the story of salvation from a white-haired old schoolmistress who was a radiant Christian. On his father's side there was much orthodox Nonconformist Christianity stemming from a generation of experience which had unfortunately become largely traditional. He never heard the gospel preached in his local church at home. Several years at two boarding schools backed with philosophical Christian teachings had made him painfully aware of the injustices in society. He had also come under the influence of what was then known as "higher criticism" which cast doubts upon the authenticity and authority of the Bible. His mind was in a muddle. Fierce temptations plagued him. Defeat and frustration were the order of the day and he hated himself for it all.

His new experience in office routine made it obvious that there was little room for those with religious convictions. His manager, who was the son of a famous evangelist, had turned aside from the Bible and become an ardent Freemason. He was staying with another member of the staff who ridiculed Christianity. To make things worse, when he suggested changing his lodgings, it was hinted that things might not go too well at the office if he contemplated a move. He enjoyed visiting some older members of the community and wished he could somehow emulate their Christian attitude to life. He loved the water and was a member of the Medway Swimming Club in Rochester. His evenings were devoted to studying for the Institute of Bankers exams.

For months he had been seeking for reality, unable to discover the source of peace and joy which his heart craved after. It was on this memorable Guy Fawkes night in 1933 that he cried after God. As he walked through the smoke laden atmosphere of this Kentish town he arrived at a clearing on the outskirts and looking up into the starry sky he cried from his heart, "O God, if You are a God, please reveal Yourself to me." The cosmic significance of the hand of the Creator always spoke to him from a starry universe. Would his heart cry be heard? Was there a God who understood and cared?

Nothing much happened during the next few weeks, but an unseen Hand was at work. Plans were being made in Head Office for a transfer. Suddenly he found himself at Goodmayes in Essex and lodgings were arranged in Ilford nearby. This was the answer to his cry. It happened like this.

One morning before leaving for the office a letter arrived in the mail inviting him to spend a weekend with a family in Tulse Hill, in South London. It was written in such a friendly way that he was delighted to accept. Little did he realise that this was the answer to his dilemma. The writer had heard of his whereabouts through friends and had accordingly shown an interest in him.

When he eventually arrived at this home he was astounded. He found the woman of the house, who had written the invitation, to be a wonderful radiant Christian. Other members of the family had also come into a real experience of Christ. The place seemed to be packed with young people who possessed an attraction which soon, made the young man realise that this was what he had been looking for! He was thrilled with these new friends and was given an open invitation to spend each weekend in this joyful atmosphere, which he was delighted to accept. On Saturday afternoons they went out together for picnics, and in the evening they went to hear such preachers as Campbell Morgan and Lionel Fletcher. On Sundays it was church with a difference as he listened to dynamic messages from Theodore Bamber at Peckham Rye. They taught him some new choruses which they sung with gusto even while they washed up the dishes. What was the secret of this exuberance? How could he enter into the same experience?

This went on for several weeks and the young man could hardly wait for the weekends to be with his new friends. They never cornered him. They never buttonholed him. They simply assumed that he was entering into their experience—at least this was how it appeared to him. He did not know how much they prayed for him!

At last the pressure became intolerable. He remembers a Saturday afternoon in Kew Gardens. Everything was just delightful but he could not enjoy anything. That was a miserable weekend. On the Monday morning just before leaving for the office, he called his hostess to one side and said, "Mrs. James, I simply can't go to work today until I have what you possess." It seemed that all his pride rose against this situation yet he had to do something about it.

A few minutes later, on the drawing-room carpet of this home, the young man who some months before, on that murky night in Kent, had called to God from the depths of his heart, now called again saying, "Lord Jesus, come into my heart. I accept you as my personal Saviour." It was the moment for which he had been born. He arose from his knees a new creature. The burden of his heart had gone as his sins were gloriously forgiven. He had begun a new life, with Christ as its very centre. There was much for him to learn in his new-found relationship, but he had begun. He had found the Saviour; and he is the one who is writing for you now! It is his earnest desire that you, too, may enter into the joy of true Christian experience.

2

A Love Story

*Who can find a virtuous woman? for her
price is far above rubies. (Proverbs 31:10)*

Until I met my wife I had never really had another girl friend.
To be true, there were one or two casual acquaintances, and
on occasions I thought I had really fallen in love. A young
nurse, converted about the same time, in association with
my friends in the Dulwich area of London, caused my head
to swim, but she wisely declined to make a firm friendship,
much to my distress and dismay at their time. There was
a relative who also made me wonder if the Lord had plans
for us for the future, but as she was a cousin I reckoned it
would be an unworkable family proposition. I determined
that as I was capable of making one of life's greatest mistakes
by marrying the wrong person, I would not carry on a love
affair until I was certain the Lord had brought the right one
into my life. This released me for opportunities to witness and

without any distractions I was able to make new discoveries in the realm of soul-winning without giving thought to any particular girl friend. I asked the Lord to bring into my life the woman of His choice in His own way and time. I would only consider an out and out Christian girl anyway. This is how it happened.

I had been staying in Redcar in Yorkshire as representative of a publishing house. My outside manager had just come to know the Lord and consequently it was a joyful occasion indeed. Then I had instructions to move to the Guisborough area. This came as a great surprise as it was a much smaller town and I questioned the wisdom of my Directors. However, having been given instructions to leave Redcar, I consequently set out one Saturday afternoon to look for lodgings in Guisborough.

I went to the Post Office for the addresses of likely boarding houses and was given three prospects. Strangely enough, I took no notice of the first on the list and wasted time looking at the others, but to no avail. Then I checked the first. It was a nice clean place in Westgate run by two sisters. I rang the bell and waited for an answer. A trim little lady answered and ushered me into the front room while she went to consult her sister. I glanced around. There was a C.S.S.M. chorus book on the piano and evidence that Christians lived here. I thought to myself, "No matter the charge, I'm staying!"

The lady returned and said it would be all right, quoting a most reasonable figure. She added, "It won't be this room as it belongs to a young domestic science teacher at the school. Yours will be on the other side of the hallway. The young lady has gone away to friends in Middlesbrough for the weekend."

I made arrangements to move in and went back to Redcar to get my bags. Strangely enough I had been boarding with two other young domestic science teachers in this place. They raised their eyebrows and looked at each other when I said I would be staying with another one in Guisborough. They knew what I didn't... that the young lady in Guisborough was a keen Christian. They also knew my stand! They told us later that they had already put two and two together!

On Monday morning, looking out of the window of my new apartment, I saw Cynthia Bruce for the first time. She was tallish with brown hair and a delightful ruddy complexion, wearing a little beret on the side of her head. I visualised a strong character deeply devoted to her work. I had only a glimpse of her and thought no more about it. Little did I realise that she supposed me to be a school inspector and was hurrying off to tidy up her domestic science block before I arrived on the scene. We laughed over this afterwards.

In the evening we were both in our respective rooms. Miss Bruce had noticed that I switched off the dance music when listening to my radio. She had also asked Miss Bowes, the landlady if she could borrow my newspaper as hers had failed to arrive. I had torn off the corner to light the fire and she wondered if I was a smoker.

After a while I realised that the young lady had gone out. Perhaps the landlady would give me permission to play the piano in her room for a while! I asked her consent, which was readily given, as I was told that Miss Bruce had gone out to play badminton and would not be back for some time. I was thoroughly enjoying myself banging out some choruses in her room when suddenly something wonderful happened. Miss Bruce had apparently gone to the post first before leaving for badminton, and unknown to us had left her racquet in the hall. She had returned for it, when she suddenly heard the piano, and bursting into the room with a radiant face she said, "Are you a Christian?" This was our first introduction. The Lord had brought it about in a wonderful way.

Well, she did not go to badminton that night. We found ourselves chatting about our Christian experience. We discovered we had so much in common. Although converted in a student campaign in Edinburgh, Cynthia had later come into the wonderful joy of full surrender through Norman Grubb of the W.E.C. This had also been my experience through the very same man of God, and the events had occurred within a day or two of each other. What a tremendous introduction this proved to be! Neither of us will ever forget that evening together. Yet it was just one of those occasions with no thought of anything lasting as a result. Just two of the Lord's people getting together and sharing Him in rich and happy fellowship.

Miss Bowes suggested that we might have our meals together, and so we saw one another quite frequently during the next few days. As I looked into the radiant face of this charming young woman and saw the strength of her character behind the musical voice which was altogether different from any I had ever heard, something was happening to me. I don't think it finally dawned until I received an unexpected letter from headquarters informing me that I was to be transferred to Hoylake in Cheshire. We had experienced something of the Lord together, yet a love affair had never entered into our thoughts. It was Christ Himself who made this friendship so rich, so wonderful, so unique. Now it was to be broken. I was going to leave Guisborough. I might never see this wonderful person again.

On that final evening as we shared Him together once more, I suddenly realised that this was the woman the Lord had prepared for me. This was to be my wonderful wife. I had never even held her hands. She had not even had a kiss on the cheek. As I left the room to assist with my packing I witnessed a little act on her part which convinced that now was the time to act. She had gently pressed to her lips something of mine before placing it into my suitcase and did not know that I had observed this token of her affection. A few minutes later I asked her to be mine and was overjoyed when without any hesitation she gladly accepted. We went out into the moonlight and there in one of Guisborough's lovely lanes we committed it all to the Lord with great joy and anticipation. I will never forget something she said to me that night. How true it has become: "I think we are going to be tested, Bob, dear." We have been sorely tried at times and our love for Him and for each other has been wonderfully strengthened as a result.

Our children often tease us and say in shocked tones "Fancy proposing to Mum after only ten days of knowing her!" Yes, that was true. However, we were engaged for some eighteen months and rarely saw each other for lengthy periods over this time. But it was in dear old Guisborough that the Lord first introduced us to each other. We met in His Name and have now been wed for thirty-five wonderful years. I feel very humbled when I think that Cynthia could have married into wealthy and influential circles, and she had declined other proposals which were most attractive, to eventually fall in love with a very ordinary person like myself. I thank God every day for such a charming wife who has had to put up with me for so long!

3

Lessons in Faith

*Seek ye first the kingdom of God and His
righteousness; and all these things shall
be added unto you. (Matthew 6:33)*

In the early days of our Christian experience my wife
and I learned many wonderful lessons of the Lord's great faithfulness which helped to reinforce our faith and determine
many subsequent decisions which would otherwise have been
impossible to make. We were very young and inexperienced,
but willing to learn more of His ways. The one great dominant
feature was the desire to do His will at whatever cost.

On our honeymoon in Richmond, Yorkshire, we were
both led to give our savings away to missionary causes and to
trust Him alone for the supply of all our needs. We had both
resigned from lucrative jobs and were intending missionary
candidates for India. We had not been accepted by any society, although our applications were being considered, so it

was entirely over to the Lord to meet all our requirements. We were standing on the threshold of an entirely new experience and were determined not to make our needs known to any man through the slightest suggestion of a hint or appeal. It was very important for us to discover how the Lord could see us through, seeing that He had directed our steps up till then.

It had not been easy to relinquish our respective positions— my wife as a fully qualified teacher and myself as a successful young business man. We had faced a measure of opposition and misunderstanding from our own circle of friends and relatives because of this, and the announcement of our wedding under such circumstances came as a shock to many, who found it inconvenient to be present. We were discovering that to do the Will of God, which broke with orthodoxy, was a costly business, not only for us but for others who could not go along with us. This was the hardest thing to bear.

Now we had given almost everything away, what was the next step? The Lord led us to spend a few days at Stockton-on-Tees, where we helped the late Mr. Hudson Pope, an old friend of the family, with a gospel campaign. Friendships were struck up as a result which have lasted to this day and Geoff Harland, then a schoolboy, is now a missionary in an area where we served the Lord in the Fiji Islands! But after Stockton what...? This was the burning question. I well remember how we spread a map out on the bedroom floor and earnestly asked the Lord to direct our steps. Perhaps we would not use these methods now, but He must have seen our longing hearts to do His will. It seemed plain to us both that we should go to Manchester, a place where we knew nobody and where we could trust Him to see us through.

We set out by bus, "not knowing whither," with two suitcases and all His promises. As we approached the city, the bus stopped for a moment right outside a church which displayed large revival notices. I was about to take our cases off the rack, thinking that perhaps this was the place of our appointment, when the bus gave a jerk and flung me back into the seat. We knew then that the Lord had other plans and continued our journey to the terminus. For the whole day we tramped the streets looking for suitable accommodation. Then in Chorlton-cum-Hardy, in Sandy Lane, we found a furnished room for only ten shillings a week. This was to be our first home and our first real experience of trusting the Lord in a new way.

The next day we decided to approach the Manchester City Mission and offer our services, which were gratefully accepted. No mention was made of finance, as it was assumed we were a young couple with independent means awaiting news of our acceptance to go to India. We were given assignments with an evangelist by the name of Mr. Valentine, and it was my nightly experience to preach the gospel in various parts of the city, accompanied by my young wife's talented voice in song.

It was not long before a stripping process began in the privacy of our own hearts as one by one items of value began to disappear. I well remember an engraved gold bracelet, given to my wife by her late father for her twenty-first birthday, going over the counter in order to keep us in food! When we had just sufficient to look respectable in the way of clothes, the Lord stepped in. The rent was due the next day and we had only about two shillings in hand. Here was the first test. We could easily give up and go back to business or teaching, but would the Lord answer our prayers? Should we continue to trust Him for tomorrow's needs? The answer was plain. We would go on with Him and see what He would do.

The very day the rent was due a letter which had been chasing us all over the country arrived with more than sufficient to meet the need. It was our first experience of this nature, and our hearts glowed with divine pleasure and anticipation. In the most remarkable ways our needs were met for the next few months. We were even paying other people's bus fares! When the food ran out we were surprisingly invited out for meals. There was no shortage of supplies, although there were certainly no luxuries. We were happily engaged in the Lord's work, often visiting the slum areas of those days and we saw quite a measure of blessing as a result.

The time came for us to leave. We had been invited south for Christmas by my people and a testimony meeting was arranged for the last night in Manchester. We had not told our story before. The time had come to declare everything. It was an unforgettable occasion. As many of the young people whom we had come to know and love listened to the story of the Lord's faithfulness, they sat spellbound. These young newly-weds, whom they had thought were affluent with independent means, had been trusting God for the supply of their needs all along! The outcome was electrifying. Many of them publicly surrendered themselves to Christ. We had actually asked for this as a sign and token from above that we were in His will. It was a memorable experience which confirmed the Lord's dealings with us in so many strange and wonderful ways, and brought much blessing to others.

In the new year we were to go to Lowick near Berwick-on-Tweed, to assist a godly minister with his vital ministry in the area. This place not only proved to be a wonderful opportunity of ministry, but it was also a Bible school for us as we sat at the feet of this godly man. We shall never forget the patriarchal appearance and flowing beard which enhanced the impression made by his consecrated life. J.A.D.J. McDonald will always be remembered by those who knew and loved him well.

To get to Lowick from the south was a problem. We had only sufficient money in hand to make our way to Guisborough in Yorkshire, where my wife used to teach, and where we originally met. We had been invited to conduct some meetings in this area amongst the young people who had been so wonderfully helped by her previous Scripture Union classes at school. I had been regarded as quite a successful young businessman and nobody knew that we had since stepped out by faith. That train journey was a nightmare. My faith was so small. Would they expect us to take rooms in a hotel, or would accommodation be provided? We had nothing left to pay for anything. How would we proceed to Lowick afterwards?

We had further wonderful lessons to learn. When we arrived we found that accommodation had been arranged, for which we were much relieved and truly thankful. There was no need to panic. The Lord had the situation well in hand.

The meetings were greatly blessed, but how about the next stage of the journey? We were both prepared to walk out of the place rather than let the Lord down. Nothing came by mail and nobody gave us a gift. Why should they? Were we not both fairly well off? On the last day at breakfast an envelope addressed to my wife was handed to us. Instinctively we knew that the answer lay inside. Patiently eating our meal, we even left off opening it until we had finished. Then the contents. It was a short note from a young lady in the area apologising for not sending a wedding present and enclosing a ten shilling note. No wedding present was more welcome. We could have hugged her for it. We would now leave with dignity. Our fare had been forthcoming.

We left by bus for Middlesbrough station, but imagine our consternation when at the booking office I asked for two tickets to Lowick. "Seventeen shillings and sixpence, please," was the reply... and I staggered. We had about seven and sixpence left now! Apologising to the booking clerk and turning to my wife I said, "Why didn't the Lord lead that young woman to put a pound note in the envelope instead of ten shillings. Now what are we going to do?"

Well, we made the amazing discovery that the bus trip was so much cheaper, that the seven and sixpence would not only provide us with tickets, but also give us some food on the way besides. If we had been given a pound, the journey alone would have swallowed the lot, and the train would have taken us several miles beyond our destination, whereas the bus dropped us right outside the manse with about twopence halfpenny left in our pockets! Surely "He sees the sparrow fall" and counts the number of hairs on our head. This was a most wonderful lesson to us of the Lord's care concerning the minutest details of our lives when we hand them over to Him. Why not trust your life to Him today?

4

Apologising for Apologies

*I am crucified with Christ: never-
theless I live; yet not J, but Christ
liveth in me. (Galatians 2:20)*

It was one of those glorious sunny days on the Nilgiri Hills in South India. After the heat of the plains, the tangy fresh air subtly scented with the delicate aroma of the eucalyptus gums is something to be experienced. We were there for the hot season, staying in a little cottage on Missionary Hill.

Our little son, Peter, was asleep in his pram in the garden. Wisps of blue smoke from the blazing gums in the hearth wafted from the chimneys, adding to the indescribable beauty and fragrance of the scene. The garden was full of lovely flowers. I can remember the red geraniums to this day. An Indian from the bazaar, with a basket full of delicious mangoes, was selling his luscious wares, another waited to bargain with his display of brass ornaments.

Suddenly the air was rent by a child's lusty cry. Our first-born was awake and exercising his lungs to advantage as he tried to tell us it was time he received some attention. Surely he would one day be a wonderful preacher! According to the book, we had learnt to take little notice of his vociferous appeals. We were able to discern the difference between a cry of pain and a demand for attention. If we picked him up at this stage we would only be asking for a sleepless night, when the performance would be repeated. Let him have a half hour's good bellowing now, and all of us would sleep like logs at night. There was wisdom in the advice we had been given by the missionary doctor's wife: "No child has ever died from a good healthy cry." The only real exercise a baby can enjoy is a fully fledged yell, which develops his lungs and expands his chest. It was now being filled again and again with this delightfully clean and healthy Nilgiri air. We continued our language study without batting an eyelid. When we had finished we would attend to our son and heir.

But someone else violently objected! Peter's daily routine happened to coincide with an old lady's rest hour. How were we to know this? An elderly woman across the way, whose afternoon siesta was rudely disturbed by our son's magnificent performance, was intensely annoyed, and it was not long before this annoyance was accompanied by criticism of those barbarous young parents whose cruelty to their children was unequalled in her estimation. Poor little chap! How could they be so heartless? He must be in agonising pain to make such a frightful noise, and they hadn't the heart to take any notice. Besides, she could not take her rest.

It was not long before we learned in a roundabout way how much she objected to us and our child's daily exercise. What right had we, mere visitors, to disturb the old resident's peaceful enjoyment? Now, if this old lady had come to us personally, I think we might have arranged for Peter to confine his yelling activities to the house instead of the garden. But her objection reached us indirectly, and if anything annoyed me it was her devious approach to the situation. Of course, I was young and inexperienced, but as far as bringing up children was concerned my wife and I were bang up to date. What did she know about these things? Didn't she realise that Peter was *our* child and that he was crying in *our* garden and that it was *our* right to bring him up in the way we thought best? Bob Stokes was a righteously indignant parent—so he thought at any rate! The only logical thing to do was to send back in a roundabout way an answer along the lines of "mind your own business," and that is exactly what happened!

Not long afterwards I felt exceedingly miserable. I knew I had done wrong. I was under the deep conviction of the Holy Spirit. For the first time I saw the old lady's point of view. There was only one way out—a letter of apology. No, no, I couldn't possibly face her in the flesh, a letter would do. So I began: "Dear Miss So and So, I'm sorry about the situation our son has created by his crying in the garden. I'm also sorry about the way I have criticised you personally, but, of course, you know that Peter is our son and that we have a right to bring him up in our way and after all he cried in our garden..."

The letter continued in this strain until it ended with a triumphant flourish of self-vindication. I had apparently succeeded in apologising and in gaining my point as well. What a victory in spiritual techniques! How marvellously the Lord undertakes!

This was just what I wanted to do... to tell her off true and proper under the guise of an apology. It was tremendous! I congratulated myself on my amazing foresight. I posted the letter with a real sense of achievement. Peter could still continue with his daily performance. She could lump it as far as I was concerned. I had at least said sorry for my remarks... even if she hadn't for hers. The matter was over as far as I could see. How little I realised it had only just begun!

A day or two later my wife found me in one of the most miserable moods imaginable. The Holy Spirit gives no peace to those who seek to vindicate themselves and I was a poor learner. I knew I had to do something about that letter. I knew that things couldn't remain as they were. I had made matters ten times worse. What could I do now to rectify the situation?

My wife asked what was troubling me.

"That old lady across the way," I said.

"Well, what do you plan to do about it?" was her next sensible question.

I said slowly and deliberately, "I intend to apologise!"

"I have never heard of anyone apologising for sending a letter of apology before," she answered with a smile.

"Neither have I," I remarked, "but I am going to do it anyway. You had better pray for me too!"

The next few minutes were agony. I made my way down the garden path to the compound across the road. As I approached the door of the old lady's home my knees almost gave way. I wished the ground would open and swallow me up. I knocked. I heard her approaching footsteps. The door opened and I saw her look of amazement as she recognised me. Before she could say anything I blurted out my apology and asked her forgiveness.

Then she started. I don't know what she said, but there wasn't much left of me after she had finished. I received the greatest telling off anyone could have ever got from anyone and when she had finished she abruptly shut the door.

It was all over. The air was fresh again. I could breathe freely. With a tremendous bound I crossed the road and flung myself into my wife's arms with a sense of joy and peace that can only come from above. I was making new discoveries. I actually liked the old dear who had been so objectionable a few minutes before. It was not long before this affection turned to love and respect, and we noticed too that she regarded us in a different light. Oh yes, we were all supposed to be real Christians. She was also a missionary, long-since retired, but how easy to let differences come between us! Now they did not exist any more, and even Peter managed to confine his preaching engagements to a more suitable time and place! It really is amazing what happens when Christ breaks through the prejudices and selfish desires of the human heart.

A few years ago I laughed when Peter asked me, out of sheer despair, "How do you bring up a family, Dad?" He is happily married with three little daughters and a son of his own now, and my wife and I often smile when we think of the way we tried to bring him up.

Maybe you are guilty of standing up for what you claim are your rights, just as I did, in a situation involving someone else's rights too. One thing we learn when Christ takes up residence in our hearts is that we no longer have any rights. They have been crucified with Him forever. The only thing is to obey Him, even if it means apologising for writing a letter of apology! I'm sure that this is what Paul meant when he said, "I am crucified with Christ: nevertheless I live; yet not I, but Christ liveth in me: and the life which I now live in the flesh I live by the faith of the Son of God, who loved me, and gave Himself for me."

5

Trial of Faith

*The trial of your faith, being much more
precious than of gold... (1 Peter 1:7)*

Truth is stranger than fiction. I want to tell you a short story
which has been a blessing to many people in different parts of
the world. It surrounds the life of a young missionary couple
in India some years ago. They came from Great Britain and
had discovered in a personal commitment to Jesus Christ the
great gift of forgiveness into a new relationship with God,
which emancipated them from a mere religious profession
which had been their background for years.

The young man was quite a successful businessman and
his wife a highly qualified and unusually talented teacher. It
was not long before their attention was drawn to the need
of the foreign mission field and they dedicated their lives
to missionary service. After a period of language study they
lived in a white-washed mud house infested with deadly

snakes and scorpions, yet they were neither alarmed nor bitten. Their faith enabled them to entrust their little son to God. Epidemics of typhoid and dysentery, together with the hazards of malaria, were faced with calm and confidence. Their work proved a blessing, and on one occasion idols were publicly burned in a nearby village. Their meagre income was a little more than seven pounds a month, but they were happy to know that they were in the will of God. In such surroundings God gave them a baby daughter as a playmate for their little son, who for some years could speak only the native language.

A few months after a visit to the hills, their little daughter, Rosemary, took sick, and was rushed to the nearest hospital, sixty miles away. There she was given every attention, while the young father visited the wards with his message of hope in a living Saviour. Within a matter of days, however, the little life began to flicker, and before they could realise it, their baby daughter was with them no more. It was a shattering blow. As they stood together over the little mound wreathed in pink oleander, they knew that the biggest test was yet to come. How could they face the Indian community back at the mission station? How could they show to those around them that Christ had risen from the dead? Where was their faith now? Would it stand the test? Did they really believe the message preached in those very hospital wards?

Turning to God in their human helplessness, they took the journey back, wondering if they would fail Him. Upon their arrival, crowds were there to greet them and the tears flowed freely. This made it all the harder, but looking to their Lord they were enabled to lift their heads high and, strengthened with His power, were prevented from breaking down as they made their way back to the bungalow. This triumph of faith had its own amazing sequel.

It happened the next day at language study where their tutor, a Brahmin, threw down his books and said, "It's no good, I can't work today... I might as well tell you that I believe."

"Believe what?" asked the young couple.

"I believe that Jesus Christ is the true and living God," was the amazing answer.

They could scarcely take it in. "What makes you believe?" they asked, with growing wonder and joy.

"Well, it's like this," answered the Brahmin. "I've been telling you about my gods for some time, but something you said about Jesus Christ has worried me a lot. You said that He rose from the dead, and I worked it out that if Jesus Christ rose from the dead, then He must be the Living God... He must be the truth. But I wanted proof. How could I know for sure? When I heard about the death of your little daughter, I said to myself, 'Ah, this is the acid test. If Jesus Christ rose from the dead I shall see it in their reactions. I shall see their faith at work.' So when you stepped off the train yesterday, I was hiding behind a banyan tree, watching to see what would happen as you walked along the road with your weeping friends. The radiance in your faces broke me up, for He did for you what my gods could never do for me. I believe He is indeed the Living God."

The years rolled by and God gave that young couple another little girl whom they called Joy in place of sorrow. She was a beautiful child. With blue eyes and auburn locks she was the joy of her parents' hearts. It was some time later, while they were serving their Master in the Godavari Delta, that the young wife was suddenly stricken with fever and was taken to hospital by her anxious husband. For weeks she lingered in a semi-delirious state with complication of typho malaria. Then the little boy came down with severe dysentery.

In desperation, the young father handed him over to the same hospital, praying that the little girl would not get the infection. In spite of his meticulous care the dreaded signs appeared and she too was a victim.

With all three of his loved ones desperately ill, the young man went to look for comfort and found it in a leper asylum nearby. Christian lepers with fingers and toes burned off by the dreadful disease were singing praises to God for His great salvation. Others, with their noses hideously eaten out, were joining in. The young man was stung to the quick. What was his suffering compared to their lot? Taking courage, he returned to the hospital, where he sensed something was wrong. Little Joy had taken a turn for the worse, and through carelessness due to a misunderstanding her body had dehydrated. His wife knew nothing of the child's illness. Only a few days before she had run into her mother's ward with much glee.

"Oh God," he cried, "Not again!" Pleading the cause of his sick wife, he was tempted to wonder whether it was worth it all... worth the sacrifice involved. Had he not left home with all its comforts? Had he not given everything, literally everything to God? As he agonised in prayer he saw thrown against the dawn of an eastern sky the starry symbol of the Southern Cross, a symbol which silenced him to submission. He bowed his head.

A few hours later, he held the frail form of the joy of his heart in his arms for the last time How could he tell his wife? Seemingly, God had prepared her heart, for she suddenly had a strange premonition that all was not well with her little darling. Now he must tell her. The next minutes are too sacred to record, for they shared them together as a husband and wife whose faith alone enabled them to overcome through the blinding tears and stabs of sorrow in the midst of pain.

It is said that the young mother insisted on the little body being brought into her ward for the funeral service. How delightful the little girl looked. She was clutching a bunch of flowers which she had always loved, and the sunlit golden curls seemed to reflect the glory into which she had entered... for as an innocent child she had sped into the arms of the One who said, "Suffer the little children to come unto Me." The mother insisted on being propped up in bed by her grief-stricken husband, and with the perspiration streaming from her emaciated body she sang with tenderness, "All for Jesus." As the young husband laid the little one to rest, the evening was filled with songs of praises and thanksgiving to the Lord of the Resurrection and the Life... a striking contrast to the hopelessness and helplessness of heathen wailing and mourning. Beautiful flowers once again symbolised the wonder of the Resurrection, and all was at peace.

The little lad recovered, but left the hospital a mere skeleton. Today he is a fine young Christian man whose life is dedicated to God. The mother, too, was nursed back to health and strength. Many years have passed. God has given the young couple three more daughters and their faith in Him, instead of waning, has grown all the stronger. Their sorrows, instead of driving them to disillusionment and despair, have deepened their love and understanding for others who have passed the same way, for they have proved the comfort and consolation of a God who in Jesus Christ suffered with His creation, as no one has ever suffered, to bring salvation, hope and joy under all circumstances, to those who repent and turn to Him.

You see, that young mother is my wife, and those wee girlies were our precious daughters!

A fuller account of this story, *More Precious Than Gold,* is available in booklet form from Trans World Radio.

6

This Is Your Car

*My God shall supply all your need
according to His riches in glory by
Christ Jesus. (Philippians 4:19)*

I shall never forget how the Lord provided transport for our
missionary representation and evangelistic work at a time when
cars in a really good condition were difficult to obtain. It was
just after the war. We had returned from India on furlough
and were staying with my people in Bridgend, Glamorgan.
The thought of waiting in bus queues and standing on bleak
railway stations in mid-winter with tedious hours of travelling,
made me realise how necessary it was to have some form of
transport to take myself and my equipment up and down the
British Isles for the next year or two. I accordingly prayed for a
vehicle, and at the same time kept my eyes open for something
suitable, without much success. They were all either worn
out or too expensive. A new vehicle was out of the question.

One day I was riding home on my father's bicycle when I saw a car approaching in the distance. It was then that I heard an unmistakable whisper, "This is your car!" It was so clear, that I was not in the least surprised when the driver stopped and went into a nearby garage. I dismounted, propped the cycle against the kerb, crossed the road and waited for him to return, having a good look at the smart little Jowett Jason which seemed to be in an immaculate condition. When the driver appeared, I was waiting for him.

"Excuse me," I said, "do you want to sell your car?" He looked somewhat confused. "Why, no," he replied. "My wife and I are on holiday. Why should we want to sell it?" Then suddenly he added, "Jump in. I'll take you around the block. Maybe we will be prepared to sell it. I'll have to consult her first, though."

I was delighted. The car went very well indeed and as to the price, well, he thought it might be worth £150. He would come back on Monday and let me know the final decision.

A night or two later I was asked to speak at a crowded meeting in a friend's home. It was a wonderful occasion. I spoke about our experiences in India and presented the needs of that great country. I had completely forgotten about the car incident in the light of the fellowship experienced in that packed drawing room. It was only as I was leaving that someone came up to me and pushed into my hand a huge wad of notes. "This is towards any need you might find necessary," he said. It was then I thought about the car. With funds in hand there was ample to pay for it on Monday. It remained a mystery as to how a man on holiday would want to part with his nice little vehicle and go back to London by train, but I remembered the clear whisper, "This is your car!" I somehow knew he would turn up.

On Monday morning as I waited in anticipation, the neat little blue car drew up outside my parents' home. The owner came into the lounge and as I carefully made out a cheque for £150 he turned to me almost in despair and said, "I don't know why I'm selling this to you. We don't want to get rid of the car, but somehow feel compelled to do so. We have to make plans to return to London by train." It was an opportunity for a witness, to tell him why we wanted the car—although he might never have understood the Lord's purpose behind the sale, unless he was converted.

And so the car was ours, to take us thousands of miles in various parts of the country during the next few years. A day or two later a friend of my father's enquired as to whether we would be prepared to sell it for profit. It was in immaculate condition, and many would have appreciated such an opportunity, but it had been kept for us in His service. Many a time I picked up young men who thumbed a ride, servicemen awaiting their discharge or serving their time in the army. Most of them heard the gospel as a result, because when I got going there was no way out of their dilemma! Travelling fast was no inducement to get out without injury. However, it was all so spontaneous, that there were few, if any, objections. The little car was proving a Godsend indeed, for it was truly sent by Him for a real purpose.

We used it to take us to camps and conferences and also for holidays. It literally groaned when we moved with our possessions to Southampton, yet it still survived. On one occasion the generator failed, but we managed to get to Scotland on the battery without having to use horn or lights. There was an occasion when it turned over on an icy stretch of road between Bath and Bristol but this proved to be an opportunity for witnessing for Christ.

It was a bleak winter morning, and I had decided to take some Christmas presents to my brother and his family in Gloucester. The road over the hills was out of the question, so I decided to travel via Bristol. Just past Smiths' potato crisp factory on the outskirts of the city, I saw a heavily laden truck coming out of an entrance on my left. Allowing time for it to slow down, I was about to accelerate again when I saw that it also had a trailer attached. This meant heavy braking. The next moment I have relived again and again. I might have been an air ace. Up and over we went, as the car slithered on an icy patch. I found myself looking at a formidable array of instruments which seemed to be upside down, as I managed to turn off the ignition. Instinct told me to jump over into the back seat, when I went through a perfectly good side window with a groan and a crash.

Suddenly daylight appeared overhead as one of the doors was opened and an ashen face looked in. It was the truck driver. He was as white as a sheet. My face, in contrast, was red with indignation.

"Why did you come out of that turning without warning?" I cried. He didn't seem to hear. Seeing me in one piece was sufficient. "Luck", he muttered "Just luck!"

I jumped out to survey the wreckage, not as bad as I had imagined. All one side was bashed in, but the car was still roadworthy. As he helped me push it back on to its wheels, he kept saying, "It's an act of God. What luck... yes, you'll get compensation for this. It's an act of God, you know."

I was ready. "An act of God?" I queried, "It's the hand of God," and quickly producing R.A. Laidlaw's excellent little booklet called *The Reason Why* I added, "and here's the reason why!" He was dumbfounded for the second time. Here was someone whom he had thought might be dead, very much alive and handing him a gospel tract! I tell you he went away reading it with tremendous interest. It was just another of those opportunities for witnessing.

The car took me safely to the outskirts of Gloucester, when one of the tyres, no doubt damaged by the accident, expired. I had to phone my brother to fetch me. A panel beater later brought the bodywork back to normal again. It was a great little car.

The years rolled by. It was time to go back to the mission field, this time to Fiji. Again the Lord did wonders. Car prices had since soared and when we parted with it I was given twice the amount we had paid for it, which helped greatly towards our expenses. The Lord knows the needs of His servants long before they do and He is always ready with delightful surprises.

We shall never realise how much that little vehicle was blessed in His service. Of course, we have had several others since, mostly second-hand, but there is a story attached to almost every one of them which proves how deeply interested the Lord is in the needs of His servants who are busy in His service.

Maybe there is a need in your life today. It may not be transport, but something which could bring much blessing and glory to His name. If so, He will meet the need. There is no question of that. It is only when we ask for things for ourselves that our prayers remain unanswered, or else we go about trying to answer our own prayers by engineering circumstances to fit that occasion. Be sure that when the Lord is busy in your life you will hear Him speak. "Thou shalt hear a voice behind thee saying, 'This is the way; walk ye in it.'"

7

Doug and Jo

Ye shall be witnesses unto Me. (Acts 1:8)

Doug and Jo lived next door to us when we were in Southampton. We had wondered who our neighbours might be, and were interested to find out that they had moved into their place only a few weeks before our arrival. They had a delightful little son only a few months old. We discovered that they were both very intellectual and that Doug's business career was implemented by flying jets in the auxiliary R.A.F.

One day my wife Cynthia beckoned to me as she watched the young housewife next door tucking up her son and heir in his pram on the lawn as she puffed away at a cigarette. Oh, how we coveted them for the Lord! What a fine young couple they would make in His service! We made no attempt to jeopardise God's opportunity for witness by putting tracts into their letter-box or button-holding them for Christ. The time would come when it was ripe. We must establish their confidence first. We must strike up a friendship as neighbours. It was more important at this stage to give the baby boy next door a birthday present than to preach to them. It is true they often wondered about us... why it was that so many young students of every nationality often visited us and propped up their cycles in the drive. Maybe we had some connection with the United Nations!

The first real opportunity for witness came when Doug was called away on business for the weekend, and my wife invited Jo to tea. We had planned everything so well... why was it that the children had to play up when she was present? No chance for a witness at all, although the young lady did raise her eyebrows when we gave thanks for our food. Apparently this initial opportunity proved more successful than we realised. Then it was Jo's turn, when I left for Capernwray Hall as guest speaker for the week. She kindly returned the invitation for my wife to visit her. When at the close Jo asked if she would return later in the evening and tell her something about our doings, it was almost too much. Cynthia put the children to bed and thanked God for such a wonderful opportunity.

It was then the test came. Having washed and polished the infants, my wife was titivating herself when she discovered to her dismay that one of the stones had come out of her engagement ring. Where could it be? What could have happened? Maybe it went down with the children's bath water? Perhaps it was in their bedclothes? Bob was no diamond merchant and could not possibly afford another stone. Oh dear, why should such a thing happen at such a time? It was then as though a voice said to her, "Why worry about an old stone? The opportunity next door is much more precious than that!" "Sorry Lord," she managed to say. "I'll go next door right away, but please lead me to the diamond in your own wonderful way and time."

She apologised for being late, explaining her dilemma, which prompted Jo to search around her furniture. Cynthia interrupted: "Don't bother to do that, dear. I've told the Lord about it, and He will lead me to the stone in good time if it is His will."

Jo was dumbfounded. "The Lord will lead her to the stone? What's all this about?" she thought, but an impact was made which was never forgotten.

They talked for hours about Christ and His wonderful claims, and Jo was becoming very interested. The situation was broken by the appearance of a young woman lodging with them, a society type of girl, who had been a debutante and was now studying physiotherapy in Southampton. Cynthia excused herself, but not before inviting young Valerie, Jo's sister-in-law on holiday, to come with her to a missionary meeting the next day. This was arranged and plans were now afoot to make real contacts for the Lord.

The next day Valerie accompanied my wife to the meeting, where Len Monies was the speaker. On their way home Valerie said, "What did Mr. Monies mean by being 'born again', Mrs. Stokes?" and my wife had the joy of explaining the new birth to this young teenager. "If you want to know any more and desire to accept the Saviour, come and see me tomorrow," she added before they parted for the night. True enough, the next day Valerie turned up and trusted Christ as her Saviour.

It was a wonderful beginning. The rest of the family did not think so however! "What's going on in that Reformatory next door? Can't they mind their own business?" The fat was in the fire all right, and things seemed to be in reverse again. How would the Lord deal with this new situation?

It happened like this. Cynthia was climbing up a small set of attic stairs, when she suddenly heard a voice which said, "The stone is here." It was unmistakable. Trembling all over, she ran her fingers along the step on which she was standing and sure enough she felt a small sharp object. Picking it up carefully and taking it to the light she discovered it was the lost diamond. "Thank you Lord," she breathed, and then running next door with the precious object in her fingers she showed it to Jo, saying, "You see, I told you that the Lord would lead me to the stone if it was His will!" You can imagine the reaction. It was all the more remarkable because the place had been swept and dusted by a cleaning woman since the loss was discovered.

Then I came home, which possibly led to the biggest reaction of all! The young couple next door were invited not only for Sunday-afternoon tea, but to the evening service at Portswood Church as well. I got Doug all alone under an apple tree in the garden and let him have everything, this time double-barrelled, while Cynthia was tackling Jo in the lounge. Mark Kagan's address on hell that evening almost made the Christians' hair stand on end, but I was thrilled to hear Doug say at the close, "I want to speak to the preacher." Imagine my horrified reaction when I discovered that he had gone to tell him off. The icy dilemma of a walk back to the house will never be forgotten. I told Cynthia to put on an extra good supper and once again the conversation turned to spiritual things. It was now or never. We closed with a reading from *Daily Light* and a short prayer, but not before I had insisted that Doug take with him a copy of *The Goodness and Severity of God* by Hart Davis. He tried to deposit it in various places but somehow I managed to retrieve it every time and hand it back to him before their departure. We said "Goodnight"— and that was that.

The next day a young red-head shot out of next door and confronted me. "I don't know whether you've got anything to do with it or not, but I've had no peace all day."

"Praise God," I replied, and she slammed the door in my face.

A few minutes later her husband came home from business, looking terrible. "Had a good day?" I asked.

"Rotten," he replied, to which I answered, "Praise the Lord!" For the second time the door was slammed in my face.

I went into the kitchen. "Things are happening next door", I said to my wife. "They are under conviction," and we rejoiced in their misery—the only time a Christian can do this as folk come under conviction of sin!

That night Jo was helping out at the hospital. Suddenly a fellow nurse, for apparently no known reason, came to Jo and testified to her about Christ in her life. The effect was electrifying. Meanwhile Doug, at home baby-sitting, was reading the book I had left in his hands the night before. His scientific mind was taking in the miracles of the Old Testament so ably expounded in this remarkable treatise, and he was beginning to come under conviction. In the middle of this his wife returned, bursting into the room to say, "There must be something in all this after all. A nurse at the hospital told me exactly the same thing as the Stokes,"—and incidentally we had never met this nurse before!

They began to fight the issue tooth and nail. Maybe they should leave this house and find another as far away from the Stokes as possible. Eventually at midnight their ammunition was exhausted. There was nothing left to do but surrender—and the two of them, Doug and his wife, Jo, yielded themselves to Christ alone in their own lounge, in front of the fire.

The next day they came to share the good news with us, and how we rejoiced together! It was not long before many others were involved—the young lady staying with them was converted, then her best friend, who brought her sister to our home, who was also won for Christ. These were followed by others including a woman who came to install a washing machine next door. Our grocer, his wife, two sons and three other members of his family also found the Lord. A chain reaction had set in which seemed impossible to stop once it had got going.

Doug and Jo are now much older, but still rejoicing in the Lord. We met them a few months ago, when it was a joy to renew fellowship together and to recount some of our experiences after many years.

8

Auntie Lennox

Give, and it shall be given unto you;
good measure, pressed down, and...
running over. (Luke 6:38)

We first met "Auntie" in Bath in 1946. When I returned home
from some speaking engagements in the north of England my
wife told me that an elderly couple had moved into the upstairs
flat. They were interesting people indeed. The old man's wife
had died in a Japanese concentration camp, and Miss Lennox
was his housekeeper. Both had been missionaries in China for
years. Now they were back, to spend the rest of their days in the
homeland. How little we knew then the events which lay behind
their coming! It was a joy to meet them, and also somewhat
amusing to see their mode of dress. As my wife commented,
"It seems as if they have stepped out of an 1880s magazine!"

The years passed and now we were living in Southampton.
Remarkably enough Auntie was being cared for by a Christian

family in the same town, the old man having died some time previously. It was one of these extraordinary coincidences of the Christian life. But the Lord was dealing with us about returning to the mission field where we had already spent several years. We were not allowed on medical grounds to return to India, but the door was opening for us to work amongst the Indian community in the non-malarial climate of Fiji. This is how the way opened out.

One night we had been reading from *Streams in the Desert* the story of the children of Israel who had been held up on the banks of the river Jordan. At God's command the priests stepped into the water as if to cross into the Promised Land and immediately the river was dammed by a landslide, enabling them to go over. Nothing would have happened had they stood on the banks until Doomsday. They had to act in faith. We knew it would cost us £400 to get to Fiji with our little family and wondered how this would be met. This was the Lord's word to us. "I believe He wants us to put our feet into the river by taking a step of faith," I said. Accordingly we wrote to the shipping company booking our passage and looking to the Lord to meet the need.

A few days later as I was cooking the breakfast—no, it isn't that I wear the apron strings, but my beloved just happened to have one of her bad heads that morning—the post arrived. I casually opened up the mail and a cheque for £400, earmarked "passages to Fiji," tumbled out of one of the envelopes. Needless to say I ruined the breakfast as I tore upstairs to my wife and said, "Look, dear, here is the answer to our prayers. Passages to Fiji have been paid for. The money has just come to hand!"

Together we handled the precious document. It had come, not from a wealthy business man but from a little soul who had nothing in this world but an old trunk of sentimental possessions. Later we heard the story of how she had suddenly come into a small legacy, and how she knelt by her bedside as she committed it all to the Lord asking what should be done with it. It was none other than the little woman who had moved into the flat above us in Bath, and who was now living not far from us in Southampton. "Give £400 to get the Stokes to Fiji," were the clearcut instructions from above. She wrote out the cheque and popped it into the letter box, telling us later that as she did so, £400 worth of happiness was hers. Now it was in our possession! What could we say? Not much, but our eyes were moist enough at any rate.

When we announced that the money had come in for our passages, some did not take kindly to the way it had come. We told the whole story without divulging the identity of the sacrificial giver. A friend came into our home and was quite indignant as he said, "My wife and I could have given it to you!" It never occurred to me then to ask him why he had not thought about it before... How we prayed that the Lord would vindicate this precious gift! Well, He did exactly that. Not long afterwards as I was walking along the street I met our little friend. With her face aglow she stopped and said, "Mr. Stokes, I have something rather wonderful to tell you. When I was led to give you the passage money I had no idea what the Lord had planned for, me. I have just received from someone in America, someone who knew nothing of the £400, a gift of £500—so I've got it back pressed down and running over!" What marvellous proof of a loving Heavenly Father's dealings with His children! Truly, "Give and it shall be given you." How gracious of Him to vindicate His servant's sacrificial giving in the eyes of others. You ought to have seen some of their faces when they knew...!

Not only did we get to Fiji, but the Lord laid it upon our hearts to take this little woman with us and to share our home with her for as long as she needed, and that is how she became known to everybody as Auntie. Auntie had lived for many years in China. Little did she think she would spend another eighteen years in the Fiji Islands. She was loved by everyone, and cared for by all. For many years she lived with us, and when we had to leave Fiji for Australia, missionary friends persuaded us to leave her behind in the warm climate where they lovingly cared for her needs as she continued to minister to theirs. One who was willing to give everything to the Lord was not neglected by Him for the rest of her earthly life.

Auntie bore a wonderful testimony for many years. Then we were informed that she was now bedridden and it was necessary for us to send for her in order to care for her needs in Australia. A converted nurse, who had found Christ through my wife's ministry, volunteered to go and fetch her at her own expense, and Auntie was given V.I.P. treatment by the air company. We met her at the airport in a wheel chair, still rejoicing in the Lord.

Auntie did not live long after that. Her testimony made a great impact upon the nursing staff at the home which was to be her last on earth. Although there was no reciprocal agreement between Australia and Fiji to subsidise nursing home expenses, the Lord looked after her needs, which were great. My wife and I visited her regularly to see that she was comfortable, and we remember a conversation just before she was taken "Home." She looked at us both, the wrinkles of her small wizened face emphasising the concern of her heart. "I wonder..." she said, "I wonder if I have withheld anything from Him." We were amazed. This little soul whose property had been ransacked in China many times, whose house had been looted and burned down, who had spent years in a Japanese prisoner-of-war camp and had emerged as a hunchback... who had given her legacy to get us to Fiji, was now saying, "I wonder if I have withheld anything from Him."

A few days later, Auntie passed peacefully away, and just a handful of Christians attended the funeral service, with fewer still at the graveside. An unknown warrior of the Cross had been called to her rest, and the reception committee on the other side must have been a very big one.

Auntie Lennox has gone to her reward. Memories of her are still precious to dwell upon. She never hit the headlines on earth, but she will be in the front ranks of the saints in Heaven. Her simple faith and devotion to the Lord, which was an inspiration to so many, is summed up in the words she herself uttered just before she was called "Home." Can we ask ourselves the same question? *"I wonder if I have withheld anything from Him?"*

9

Missing the Boat

My times are in Thy hand. (Psalm 31:15)

We often hear the phrase "missing the boat," but I suppose few of us realise what this means in actual experience. I did not realise the significance of this until it actually happened to us about twenty years ago on our way to the Fiji Islands. Let me tell you of an incident in our lives which at the time seemed quite disastrous, but which proved to be a blessing.

We were on our way to Fiji via Australia on the old P. and O. liner *Otranto*. The weather was perfect as we approached Fremantle early one morning with great anticipation. This would be our first glimpse of Australia. I shall never forget my reaction as we saw some of the grain elevators looming large on the horizon. We were prepared for a day in Perth, where we planned to visit an evangelist who was running a canteen in the centre of the city. His name had been given to us by friends in Ceylon. Many people on the ship wondered how it was we had friends in every port, something very precious to the Christian as he travels from place to place. Truly the fellowship of the Lord's people is wonderful.

It was going to be a hot summer day, so we dressed as lightly as possible in order to enjoy it to the full. We soon found our friend, Stan Drew, who was delighted to meet us, and we enjoyed some refreshment together. As we left the canteen, something happened to change the whole day for us, something we had not foreseen at all. Our little girls decided to clean up Perth by wiping their hands a long some of the shop fronts until they were black with dirt. My wife insisted on taking them back to the canteen wash, and it was then that everything began to happen.

Our evangelist friend had been on the phone to a local Christian business man telling him of our visit, and he immediately offered to take us out. We had left by this time, so Stan tore up the road only to go in the opposite direction. He was slowly returning, having given up hope of seeing us again, when we turned up on the steps of the canteen. We were then told to wait for this business man who would be pleased to come in his car and entertain us for the day. How wonderful! People we had never met before would show us round, and save us much foot-slogging in the heat.

It was a wonderful day. The children were treated to ice-creams and we visited many beautiful areas of the lovely city of Perth before it was time for us to leave. As we thanked our friend for his kindness, I looked at my watch and casually said, "The ship leaves dead on time. Perhaps we ought to make our way back to the docks?"

"Have no fear on that score," he answered. "I've been meeting the ship for twenty years and we haven't missed one yet!" That sounded reassuring enough and we thankfully left the situation in his hands.

On our way back we were so engrossed in a conversation that we were startled when he said, "Oh, I've forgotten. There's a short cut to the wharf which will save us time." We turned off the main road and were soon heading for the *Otranto,* which we saw a short distance away. Folk were streaming towards it behind the iron railings in front of us. We were in good time to make it. Then we got a rude shock. The gate into the wharf was closed and locked. Our friend exclaimed in dismay, "It's the dockers' annual holiday! We can't get through here, we must return to the main road and go through the town instead."

When we found our way to the busy intersection in the rush hour, there seemed no possible way through. It was minutes before we could proceed. Slowly crawling into town we headed to the wharf from the opposite direction. The car shot on to the quay and we all tumbled out in a panic. I grabbed one of the children, my friend another, and my wife followed with the third. A tremendous cheer went up from the ship from stem to stern. Could we make it? I was suddenly aware of the fact that the gangplank had been withdrawn. Passengers urged me to run to the stern, which was still rubbing against the side of the dock, and where there was a huge open doorway in the side of the steamer. As I approached I could see a widening gap. Maybe I could jump this with one of the children, but by the time the rest of the family arrived it would be too late for them. I wisely decided against this procedure.

Suddenly we were approached by two strange men, tugmasters so I was told. "Get into this car," they urged. We did so, and the next minute we were tearing along the wharf, with our friend following in pursuit. We had hardly recovered from the shock of missing the boat when we heard the shriek of a whistle, and the next minute we were stopped by a speed-cop for exceeding the speed limit. This was too much! As he listened to our plight, the cop obligingly put away his notebook and joined with us in the chase for a launch to take us to the ship. Normally this I would have been successful, but it was the dockers' annual holiday and there was not a boat or a man available. They dropped us near a jetty and went off to look for some help, in the meanwhile the ship was slowly turning in the harbour, and would pass this spot within the next few minutes. What could we do? I thought of the awful predicament we were in, stranded in Perth with the next stop, Adelaide, 1,100 miles away. All our personal effects in the cabin lying loose or in drawers, and our ultimate destination, Sydney, another 1,000 miles beyond that! What was going to happen?

The tugmasters returned and said they had hit on a plan. They would signal to an approaching tug which would pull alongside, and pick us up. Then we would transfer to the pilot boat, and from there, climb the rope ladder up the moving ship to safety. We had no idea what it was like to climb a rope ladder with children on our shoulders up the slippery side of a moving ship. Perhaps it was just as well! However, as the tug approached, it mistook the signal and simply tooted in reply and veered off. We were then told there was no other way, and thanking our would-be helpers for their trouble we waved to the crowds on the ship and I took a photograph as well... a photograph of what it really means to "miss the boat."

Our Christian friend then told us to jump in his car and we would make our way to the station and get a train to Adelaide. It would arrive just before the ship departed again for Melbourne. Just imagine a couple of nights in a train without any suitable clothing or blankets!

As I approached the booking office and asked for tickets, the clerk replied, "Sorry, no bookings available for three weeks. This is the holiday season, you know!"

By this time my face was as white as my shirt. Our friend said, "Don't worry, Bob, the Lord will see you through."

"Yes," I replied. "I was just wondering how He was going to do it, that's all."

His answer will never be forgotten. "You are going to come home with me," he said. "My wife and I will entertain you for a couple of days, and then we will put you on a Skymaster plane at my expense in good time to pick up the ship in Adelaide. It was my fault you missed the boat, and I will take the money out of my business, something I could not have done a few years ago."

We were driven to his home and warmly welcomed by his wife, who immediately obtained clothing for the children. It proved to be a wonderful time of rich fellowship indeed. We contacted our friends on the ship, and all was well. Later we discovered that in the notorious Bight the ship hit the only really rough sea since leaving England when almost everyone was sick, and besides that the stewards were rolling drunk after their day in Fremantle. We were on dry land and enjoying wonderful Christian fellowship!

Our adventures were not over by any means. The Skymaster plane hit a tropical storm, which was quite an experience. When we landed in Adelaide, friends who had been contacted from Perth took us out for the day, and we found we were cut off by a bush fire. We wondered if we would miss the ship for the second time! However, all was well and we had a wonderful story to tell to those on board. We learned later that if our air flight had not been paid for, the passengers were prepared to pass the hat around the ship to make their contribution, one of the results of our taking a Sunday School on board for their children. Another thing-if the ship had docked a few days later, the plane which we would have boarded would have taken us with it to our deaths. It crashed with the loss of all lives shortly after take-off-one of Australia's worst air disasters. Surely we can learn much from this experience. We can testify to the fact that "our times are in His hands;" that God's minute hand as well as His hour hand are perfectly timed. There is really no need to panic. Our experience exercised a Christian's heart, created wonderful Christian I fellowship, made a unique Christian opportunity for witness, and increased our own Christian faith. It was indeed one of those "All things" that "work together for good to them that love the Lord, who are called according to His purpose." But my friend, when it comes to the question of Eternal Life, be sure *you* do not "miss the boat."

10

Her Jewel Box

*The way of transgressors is hard (Prov-
erbs 13:15)... [but] the meek He
will teach His way (Psalm 25:9)*

It was an unforgettable time of blessing and challenge at a Christian convention in New Zealand. I had been sharing messages with
a man whom God was greatly using-Gordon Blair, whose ministry
among the troops in Singapore had been singularly blessed of God.
Gordon was later used to establish the Emmaus Bible School in
Sydney, Australia, which was afterwards dedicated to his memory.
It is now some years since he was called Home to his eternal reward.

As a result of this ministry, there was much confession of sin
and subsequent getting right with God. We saw scores whose
lives were gloriously changed as a result, and the story of one
man in particular stands out in my mind.

This man had come to both Gordon and me independently
for personal counselling after a terrible time of heart searching.

His life was one big mess. Immorality, to depths of degradation that almost made us sick, came to light in these private conversations. We both gave him the-same advice unknown to each other. We both told him that the only way back to God, apart from the cleansing which Jesus Christ affords to those who truly repent, was to tell his Christian wife the kind of life he had been living and ask her forgiveness. He was driven mad by the thought of such a confession. It would kill her. We told him he should have thought of that before, as he had sinned both against her and against God.

The pressure was on. He came to both of us time and time again, only to be given the same advice. I shall never forget the moment when he sobbed like a child and broke down completely. The Lord was getting through to his wicked heart. He knew such forgiveness as he had never known. Now it was up to him to make restitution to his lovely little wife. How could he do it?

Something happened in one of the meetings to make this gloriously possible. His wife came under conviction over some very insignificant thing compared to his sin, and as her heart was prepared by the Lord to make amends, she rose from her seat at the close to go outside. Seeing her state of brokenness, her husband followed. It was then that he asked her forgiveness, which was so freely given. "If the Lord has forgiven him, so do I," she told me afterwards.

We were amazed at the grace of God. We thanked Him for such magnanimous love. It was a reflection of Calvary. The change in their home life was indescribable. They even adopted a family to make the picture complete. For many years they have rejoiced in His goodness and praised the Lord for His victory. Their witness has been outstanding. Nobody would dream of what the past had been.

It was a few weeks after this wonderful reconciliation that I visited their home. To see their gratitude of heart and to share in their Christian hospitality was a tremendous experience. We praised God together for what He had wrought and thanked Him again and again for the precious cleansing of the Blood of Jesus Christ.

It was then that something happened which really stirred my heart. In front of her husband, this lovely Christian woman who had so freely forgiven him, produced her jewel box and handing the precious contents to me said, "Mr. Stokes, please accept these as a token of gratitude to the Lord for restoring my husband." I fingered them reverently as I recognised their worth in His sight. Such sacrificial giving is rare. Once again I marvelled at the matchless grace of God. A thank offering such as this must surely bring blessing to many, but what was I going to do with it?

For several weeks these jewels were carried in my brief case as I sought the best means of disposing them. I wanted their highest value for Jesus Christ. A dealer might only give the barest minimum, whereas I desired the maximum for the Lord.

At last my opportunity came. It happened like this:

I was speaking at another conference, mostly attended by New Zealand farmers and their wives. It was the time for a fresh challenge. I spoke of the mission field and its needs. I challenged those prosperous farmers concerning their giving to those who were labouring in God's harvest fields. I spoke of the millions across the seas who had never heard, who were without Christ and without hope in this world or the next. Later I was told that many of those men who listened to me were renowned for their tight fists as far as God's work was concerned. Then I told the story of the woman and her jewels. I spoke of the way in which her husband had been gloriously cleansed and restored and how she gratefully gave of her best as a thank offering to the Lord. I was surprised at the way in which the Lord gave me such liberty to throw out

the challenge to an audience now spellbound as they listened
to the message.

The time had come to act. I then did something unprecedented in my ministry—something I had never done before
and have never repeated since. I called for an offering box.
To this day I can see eyebrows raised as I dared to break with
orthodoxy. The box was produced and handed to me in the
pulpit. No plans had been made for a collection. What would
happen now? Every face was riveted to mine with attention.

First I said that we would take an offering for the cause of
the Lord overseas. Then I dropped the jewels one by one into
the box, challenging those present to emulate the example
of this Christian woman. Next I endorsed a cheque which
had been given to me before the service towards my personal
expenses and popped this into the box as well. The result was
electrifying. I had no axe to grind. The jewels were for the
Lord. Someone could value them and add this to the offering.
It was a time for multiplication.

Needless to say, that box was filled to overflowing with gifts
for the Lord's servants. I forget the amount given, but I understand it was one of the largest offerings ever received in that
place for His work overseas. The woman's jewels had at last
found a market where their value would be enhanced. They
had challenged His people to give sacrificially to His cause.
They had found a response from warm hearts. His Name had
been once more glorified.

I wonder if this story is being read by someone who is
"close-fisted" like those prosperous farmers. You may have a
large bank account which is never broken into by the urgency
of the Lord's work on every side. Maybe this story of the Christian woman's response of gratitude to the Lord for restoring her
husband will speak to you as you review the whole situation
of your giving to His cause. You may even be someone like

that husband. He professed to be a Christian when his life was indescribably wicked and immoral. He realised things could not continue as they were, but how could he put matters right? God gave him the opportunity just at the right time, and He will do exactly the same for you too, if you will come to Him for cleansing and seek His way of restitution. Remember, "the way of the transgressor is hard," but it is worth it in the end. There are no short cuts in the way back to God from the dark paths of sin.

11

A Couple of Chairs

*Come unto Me, all ye that labour
and are heavy laden, and I will
give you rest. (Matthew 11:28)*

The auction was in full swing, and the bidding was brisk. Most of us missionaries in Fiji bought our furniture this way, and whenever anyone was leaving the colony it was announced that their property was up for sale. It was an occasion for the local auctioneer to get busy. He was an interesting old character, and the auctions took place in the homes of those who were selling up. It was quite a social rendezvous, coloured by the presence of Indians, Chinese, Fijians and Europeans. We always enjoyed the fun.

On this occasion we wanted a couple of easy chairs and spotted what we thought were a nice pair, unholstered in an attractive green cloth. They we eventually knocked down to us for a very reasonable price, However, one of these chairs was occupied by a young woman expecting her first child, and when we came to take it away we found that the springs were sticking through the upholstery! These had been carefully concealed by her anatomy. How we laughed together over this discovery.

This was our first introduction to Gordon and his wife, a young couple recently arrived in the colony from New Zealand. As we discovered that they lived quite close to us, we offered to take some of their furniture in our van, and a friendship was struck up which undoubtedly paved the way for real blessing. Gordon was a brilliant young journalist and we were able to witness to him and his wife, although he later admitted that whenever he came to our home he was anxious to get away before the conversation turned to spiritual things! We shall never forget how proudly he announced the birth of their little daughter when he came to our home one evening. How we rejoiced with them in their new found joy! His wife's parents and sister had also come from New Zealand to be with them at this time. It was a family reunion for a very special occasion.

But you can imagine how we felt when a telephone call early the next morning from the hospital informed us that the baby had mysteriously died during the night. Would we be the conveyor of the bad news to Gordon and his family? Would we kindly tell them as soon as possible?

I suppose this is one of the hardest things to do in life, and it was with a very heavy heart that I dressed and made my way to their little home not far away. I could see Gordon through the bedroom window as I approached, and my presence at such an early hour must have prepared him for the worst. It was not long before the whole family were sharing in his sorrow. There is not much one can do under such circumstances. We could only commit them lovingly to our Heavenly Father. I left them alone with their broken hearts, praying that the Lord would undertake.

Gordon's wife reacted so violently to the news of her baby's death that a fever set in, and she was declared dangerously ill. His mother-in-law took it so badly that they had to carry her out of the hospital in hysterics. Within a very short time the young mother succumbed to the whole situation and passed away, leaving every one literally stunned with shock. To think that this young man should lose both his wife and daughter within the space of a few short days, when the pregnancy had been normal, was unbelievable! We have often thought about this. Was it mere coincidence that my wife had visited her frequently and given her many flannel-graphs to cut out for our Sunday School, illustrating in simple clear terms the way of salvation? God moves in mysterious ways His wonders to perform. We heard evidence that during this young mother's delirium there were definite indications that she was ready to go. She actually said that Christ was calling her home. But the aftermath! Some of us will never forget those dreadful moments when Gordon knelt between the two newly-dug graves and prayed for the first time in his agonising dilemma. We will never forget how he removed his wife's photograph from the wall, running his fingers through his hair as he just looked and looked at her again and again. A missionary friend and I stood by and wept. It was all we could do. How could we possibly enter into his feelings at such a time?

The days and months passed by. His wife's parents left shortly after the funeral for their home in New Zealand, but his sister-in-law stayed on in Fiji. We often had her to our home, little realising what the outcome would be. It was not long afterwards that she definitely accepted Christ as her own Saviour and Lord. In the meanwhile, Gordon did everything to try and drown his sorrow. Drinking did not seem to alleviate the situation so he took to studying Hinduism. There was still no answer to his problem. Tossing one night on his bed in an agony of mind he suddenly remembered the words of our Lord which at some time or another he must have heard: "Come unto Me all ye that labour and are heavy laden, and I will give you rest." It was just like that. In a flash he turned to the Lord and everything changed. He was gloriously converted. His sister-in-law, knowing nothing of this, went to tell him that she had become a Christian. Can you imagine her reactions when he calmly said "I, too, have come into the same experience." So convinced was he that his mother and father-in-law should know what had happened, that he paid for my wife's return fare to New Zealand to accompany his sister-in-law when she left Fiji, and it was a wonderful opportunity for a further witness. Gordon left the entire staff of the local press speechless with his new found experience. He departed shortly afterwards for Australia, but an impact had been made which will never be forgotten by those who knew him. The years rolled by. Gordon has remarried and is very happy with his little family in Sydney. It is some time since we have seen him, but imagine my reactions when, travelling on an old Italian liner from Melbourne to Genoa a year or so ago, I met up with his cousin and her family who boarded the ship in Singapore! This was a further opportunity to witness. I had never met her before, but when I mentioned during casual conversation that I had spent many years in Fiji, the matter came to light. So God has ways and purposes beyond our understanding in getting the truth of the gospel into the hearts of those who might otherwise never hear.

Little did we realise that a visit to an auction would lead to a friendship which would help to soften the blow of a bereavement and pave the way for the conversion of precious souls. Ordinary events can be interwoven into a glorious pattern of divine origin, and contacts made which could never come about otherwise. This makes the humdrum exciting, and takes the drabness out of life. It is backed by those amazing words, "All things work together for good to them that love God, who are called according to His purpose." A couple of old chairs started the chain reaction of this interesting story. What could set things going in your direction today?

12

Ted of Savusavu

*Go home to thy friends, and tell
them how great things the Lord
hath done for thee. (Mark 5:19)*

My wife and I went to visit a dear woman whose husband had
been unfaithful to her. She would not divorce him because, she
said, "I married him for better or for worse, and to give him
what he wants now would be merely to play into his hands."
It was a sad story. Teena had been wonderfully converted. Her
children attended the same school as ours in Suva, Fiji, and she
was a radiant Christian. She loved the Lord and was a regular
member of our church fellowship.

Our visit that morning was different. We found that she
already had another visitor, who was delighted to meet us. He
told us his story.

Ted came from the island of Vanua Levu, where he had
worked on his father's copra estate. For some years he had been

in New Zealand, and he had also represented Fiji at the Olympic Games in England. His people, who were very religious, often attended church, but their lives were riddled with sin. Drunkenness and debauchery were often mixed with religious devotion. Ted found the Lord in New Zealand while walking along one of Auckland's streets. Hearing some music coming from a building nearby he dropped into a mission hall to be gloriously converted. This changed the entire course of his life. He had since spent some time in a Bible School in Australia.

The burden on his heart was for his people along the Savusavu coastline of Vanua Levu, so he returned to Fiji hoping to lead many of them to the Lord. "A prophet is not without honour, save in his own country," so he found it almost impossible to convince them of the truth. They knew he was different, but it just wasn't for them. So he planned with a heavy heart to leave them and to settle down for a time in England. He was actually on his way that morning and had decided to call at Teena's house as he passed through. However, he felt that he just couldn't continue his journey. The faces of his loved ones at the wharf haunted him, and he knew he ought to stay with them when they so much needed the Lord. He was sharing this burden with Teena when we turned up.

As I listened to his story I felt a tremendous urge to accompany him back to Savusavu. His testimony needed reinforcement, and perhaps the Lord was asking me to go over there and preach the gospel. I had never been before, and fairly glowed with anticipation as he shared this burden with me. It just wasn't possible to accompany him back, but it was decided that I should make a visit within a matter of weeks. So Ted, instead of continuing his journey to England, returned to his people in Savusavu. I went home with my wife to pray about the situation.

The next few weeks were dogged with all kinds of problems. Isn't this often the case when the Lord is about to do something wonderful? When I actually found time to go, I didn't have the funds to pay for the trip. In fact it became quite embarrassing to try and explain the delay to folk who were expecting me to leave, without divulging the situation. Eventually the Lord laid it upon the heart of one of the local Christians to procure the ticket which enabled me to fly to this part of Fiji.

I shall never forget that first flight over the coral seas and waving palms to Savusavu, a journey which has been repeated many times since. The shimmering blues and greens of tropical lagoons set in their golden frames of coral were breathtaking and my camera clicked again and again. Little did I realise that I would be showing these pictures in many parts of the world to illustrate the significance of a trip which was never to be forgotten in many ways.

The ride in a truck from the airport, which had been cut out of a coconut plantation, took me along a winding coastal strip under waving palms skirting magnificent coral beaches. It was indeed a reminder that "something lives in every hue Christless eyes have never seen;" a place where "every prospect pleases, and only man is vile." I was given hospitality in the home of one of the planters and meetings were to start the next day and continue for at least two weeks. It was all so wonderful that I went off to sleep that night thanking the Lord for this rare opportunity.

I was rudely awakened by the sounds of shouting, cursing and the breaking of glass. The men had returned from the hotel much the worse for drink and this was the usual Saturday night performance. As I listened to the pandemonium I felt very uneasy. How could such a people come under the impact of the gospel. Would they even listen? I prayed for much wisdom, asking the Lord to undertake in His own wonderful way.

Ted soon joined me to pray for his people and to arrange some meetings in the area. All available copra houses along the coast were commandeered for this purpose, and to my amazement they were filled to capacity as night after night I hit out against sin with all the deadly denunciation of God's Word. These people didn't have to be told what sin was, but they were keenly interested to hear what God had to say about it. I was amazed. Night after night they came, but I made no public appeal. The time was not yet ripe. The conviction had not gone deep enough.

It was during the second week, when I began to lift up Christ as God's answer to sin and all its problems, that God broke through. The first to respond was a woman whose home provided a regular weekend of drunkenness. How wonderful to be able to record that this home was later used to celebrate the Lord's supper. Then others followed, including her husband. It wasn't long before the telephone lines ran hot with the news. Conversations were rudely interrupted on the party line with cries of "Are you saved yet...?" Before the end of the week some twenty or more of the roughest and toughest copra planters and their wives had found the Lord. One man put up the banns to marry the girl he had been living with for years.

In certain quarters, opposition became quite firm. The news reached Government headquarters in Suva. It could not be denied that something unusual was going on, and that a people whom the police had been unable to control were becoming law-abiding citizens. They were given six weeks to revert to their former ways, but now fifteen years have passed! A little church on a hill for all the tourists to see is a memorial of what the Lord did in these memorable days. Ted's testimony had at last got through to his people.

One young man, Thomas, and his wife Grace, need special mention. Thomas had spent some £5,000 on drink in ten years.

His weekly copra yield, amounting to about £80 in those days, was squandered in drink leaving only a few pounds for his wife. Thomas had tried again and again to mend his ways. Being a cut above the average, and lighter skinned, he was looked up to by the rest. I will never forget when Thomas came to the Lord. It was not in Savusavu but in Suva at the bedside of his wife during her confinement. He knelt with me and simply said, "Lord Jesus, save me from my sins. I accept you into my heart as my own personal Saviour." Many times Thomas had tried turning over a new leaf, to no avail. Now he was receiving a new life, which makes all the difference. Thomas and Grace have not looked back and their testimony has rocked the community. Government officials commented on the way his estate was tidied up shortly after his conversion.

Today there are missionaries in Savusavu following up this work, and I know they would value your prayers. If ever you are in Fiji then you know just where to go for a precious time of fellowship, made all the more wonderful by South Sea Island hospitality and tasty delicacies that are just out of this world!

13

Over the Reef

...that through death He might...
deliver them who through fear of
death were all their lifetime subject
to bondage. (Hebrews 2:14, 15)

In the over-ruling providence of God, many of us have no
doubt had many wonderful deliverances from disastrous consequences which could have led to an untimely death. As I look
back over my life, one event in particular comes readily to
mind. It happened in the Fiji Islands during a time of rich
blessing amongst the copra planters, on the island of Vanua
Levu. A missionary friend and I were offered a lift along the
enchanting coastline by a young man who had recently come
to Christ. He was taking his boat to another plantation and
suggested that we did some fishing on the way—not inside the
reef, but in the deep blue waters outside, where it was possible
to troll for barracuda, an excellent proposition.

We were delighted. The prospects seemed good, and there was a cloudless sky which promised calm waters. As we set off leisurely and entered into the Pacific Ocean outside the coral barrier we prepared our lines for a good catch, and it was not long before we were well rewarded. The barracuda is a dangerous fish to handle, but when he is played out by the speed of the launch, there is not much to worry about. We had quite a few dead fish swilling around in the bottom of the boat in next to no time, and greatly anticipated a delicious meal cooked in native style in *lolo*— the milk of the coconut, flavoured with chillies and wild ferns, which adds to the delicacy of the flavour. Believe me, there is nothing so tasty as sea food cooked in South Sea Island style!

We were so engrossed in our fishing that we had not noticed an ominous sign on the horizon. A storm cloud had appeared, no bigger than a man's hand, but with the tremendous pressures that build up, it soon developed into a tropical squall. When we first noticed it, we thought it would blow in the opposite direction, but it gradually changed its course and headed right for us. Within minutes, circumstances changed. Wind puffs, increasing in force, converted the placid ocean into an angry sea. Blue skies gave place to ominous clouds. We were in a dangerous position, just outside the reef, with no shelter or safety for another four or five miles.

As we rocked and rolled, the boat was filling up, not only with tropical rain, but also with the ocean, as waves and spray broke over the sides. We frantically began to bale out, only to realise that we were attracting sharks to our vicinity with the blood of the fish we had caught, which had mixed with the water in the boat. Then the inevitable happened. A huge wave swamped the outboard motor, which put it out of action. We were now at the mercy of the sea, slowly drifting towards the reef which was being pounded by the breakers. We could never make the safety of the lagoon in time.

It was then I began to do some furious thinking. This might be my last moments on earth. If we were smashed up against the reef we would sink, that was for sure, and the chance of scrambling over that razor-sharp barrier was remote. Men who had been bashed against the coral and survived had spent months in hospital fighting the poison which prevented the ugly lacerations from healing.

As I sat in the prow of the boat looking for signs of an opening in the reef, I thought of many unusual things. Naturally I remembered my wife and family, and what it would mean to them to be without a husband or father. I then thought of many letters which I ought to have written... how strange! Things which had been quite insignificant now loomed large. It was quite an experience. Would I eventually drown or be attacked by a shark? Would I succumb to the cruel fangs of the poisonous coral? I was now drenched with rain and spray. To lighten the boat we had jettisoned everything overboard, including a shipment of coconuts. The face of the young man who was an experienced fisherman was as white as his shirt. My missionary friend looked grim.

As we were slowly but surely driven helplessly towards the pounding waves breaking over the reef, our young friend tried to make himself heard.

"Can you both swim?" he shouted.

We both nodded.

"Then forget the boat... forget everything else... and make for it," he yelled.

I carefully put my camera into an airtight Glaxo tin with the hope that it might drift ashore, and poising myself for the plunge, I was about to prayerfully hurl myself to the mercy of the elements when I felt a heavy hand on my shoulder.

"Wait, Bob," my missionary friend said with an air of confidence.

I looked behind me and saw an enormous wave approaching. I was fascinated. As it grew bigger and bigger it suddenly curled under the boat and before we realised what had happened it had carried us completely over the reef, depositing us in the calm lagoon the other side.

"It's a miracle... it's a miracle!" cried the young man who had only recently come to know the Lord.

We were now safe. The elements could rage, but once in the calmer waters of the lagoon we were no longer in danger. As we looked at each other and gave thanks to God for His wonderful deliverance, we all started to tremble from head to foot with reaction from the situation.

We were now able to paddle and push the boat through the lagoon for two miles until we reached our destination. When our friends saw us approaching, it was also a real testimony to them, as they too had just come to know the Lord.

One of them said, "You have never come through that storm!"

"We certainly have!" was our reply, and we all gave thanks to the Lord for a mighty deliverance.

It was the experience of a lifetime, one we shall never forget. As we drank some delicious hot drinks prepared for us by our dear friends we were grateful to be spared to serve the Lord for some time longer, although had our time come we would have been "absent from the body and present with the Lord".

I wonder if these words are being read by someone who has no certainty of the after-life, no joy of anticipation when life has ended on earth. The Bible says that some people are in bondage all their lives because of this. Just listen to Hebrews 2:14, 15: "Forasmuch then as the children are partakers of flesh and blood, He also Himself likewise took part of the same; that through death He might destroy him that hath the power of death, that is, the devil—and deliver them who through fear of death were all their lifetime subject to bondage." There is no need to fear death any more. Christ died for our sins to make forgiveness possible: to make it a reality in our everyday experience. When we accept the risen Christ into our lives by faith, He comes in the mighty power of His Spirit to dwell in our hearts. He gives us the witness of His Spirit and a newness of life which is eternal. "For God sent not His Son into the world to condemn the world, but that the world through Him might be saved... For God so loved the world that He gave His only begotten Son that whosoever believeth in Him should not perish, but have everlasting life." Remember, "He that hath the Son hath life, but he that hath not the Son of God hath not life."

When I sat in the prow of that boat, I knew that because Christ lived in me, I would live forever with Him. The eternal Purchaser and Possessor of my soul would not let me go when the time had come to leave my earthly tabernacle! My friend, you too can know this great experience. You can know it right now, if you will only come to Him by faith, and then come what may (you will have to leave this scene one day), you will be secure in His safe keeping forever. The alternative is too terrible to contemplate. Thousands are going to a lost eternity because they will not have anything to do with Christ. You need not side with them. Do something about it before it is too late. Do something right now. Accept Him into your heart as your own personal Saviour and Lord, when you will become safe and cure for all eternity.

14

Dave's Conversion

*If any man be in Christ, he is a
new creature: old things are passed
away; behold, all things are become
new. (2 Corinthians 5 :17)*

Dave was employed by the C.S.R. sugar mill in Lautoka, Fiji.
His upbringing had been deplorable. He was a weak- willed
profligate who indulged in drinking, gambling and wife-beating.
One day Dave's wife came to me in great concern. "Can you
please do something for my husband? Can you get him to change
his ways? Life is becoming intolerable as he beats me up every
day." I listened to this poor woman's pathetic story. Of course,
we would do our best to influence him. We would certainly visit
him, but there was no guarantee that we could get him converted.
This was the work of God. We would see what could be done.

I was staying with my dear missionary colleague, Alan
Packer from New Zealand, and we decided to pay Dave a

visit. Maybe we went more than once or twice, but without any response. It was not as though we had not prayed for Dave. We knew the situation all too well. It was certainly a case for God's intervention. But would Dave listen? Would he heed God's warning? Would he respond to the claims of Christ?

One night after we had spent a considerable time pleading with Dave to come to the Lord something wonderful happened. We did not ask him whether he believed in Jesus Christ or not, because we knew that even if he did it would make no difference to his life. Too many give mental assent to the truth which has no effect whatsoever. Even the devils believe, but they tremble! We placed before him the solemn aspect of continuing in his sin with ultimate judgement and damnation, or else repenting and receiving the Lord Jesus Christ in his heart. We did not challenge him in the realm of his intellect, but in the sphere of his will. "Will you receive Him? Will you repent of your sin?"

For sometime Dave hedged every approach made in this way. Finally, around midnight, in his own little home under the shelter of the Lautoka sugar mill, Dave said those wonderful words that have brought millions out of darkness into light. "I will!" There and then he repented of his evil ways and accepted into his heart by faith the Lord Jesus Christ. We went home rejoicing with him and his new found faith. How glad and happy his wife would be now that Dave was converted!

Nothing could be further from the truth. A day or two later I was approached by an infuriated wife. "What have you done with Dave? Why have you changed my husband?" he stormed.

Oh, yes, Dave was changed all right. His drinking, swearing and wife-beating had miraculously stopped. His pals were amazed at the change. Even a Fijian policeman asked me what had happened to him. The news of his conversion had spread everywhere. He was indeed a new man in Christ. This weak-willed man had already become a strong character in his radiant testimony for God. Now his wife was furious. I have rarely met a madder woman. So infuriated was she, that after she sent for me I had to sit outside the veranda of her home and listen to her abuse as she threw butt-ends of cigarettes at me in between the storming sessions.

At last I managed to get a few words in: "But, why are you so ungrateful? Why are you so furious now that Dave is converted? Hasn't he stopped beating you up?"

"Oh, yes," she replied, "He's stopped beating me up, but the old fool has turned religious. He won't even have a little drink with me now. He's reading his Bible instead!"

So that was it. She wanted him reformed but not regenerated. She wanted him toned down but not completely changed. She wanted him to enjoy the old life without its abuses or excesses. She did not want her husband a man of God! It was good that he had stopped beating her up, but it was terrible that he had become religious. She was furious.

Now the tables were turned. She started to beat him up! One day when he returned from the mill she tore his tomato plants out of the ground, roots, fruits and all, and flung them around his neck. But Dave did not retaliate. He now loved his wife. He prayed for her. He bore her abuse with patience and it all paid off. Some time later she too accepted the Lord and now they are both in Queensland, Australia, witnessing together to His saving grace and power in their lives.

Dave and his wife are now at peace, for the peace of God rules in their hearts. I have often thought of their story and how true to life it is. So many people have no objection to God breaking into their lives to alleviate a certain situation but "so far and no further." Their cry is that of old: "We will not have this Man to reign over us." We don't mind going to

Heaven at His expense, provided we don't have to change our way of living. We don't mind if He saves our children from sickness, provided He doesn't save their souls from sin. We have no objection to going to church once in a while, provided we can still have our drinking parties. This is the cry of the world. Reformation, not regeneration. An outward change, but not an inward experience. Save us from the unpleasant things, but give us liberty to enjoy sin for a season.

Dave was one of the weakest-willed men I have ever met, yet he demonstrates the power of the cross of Christ in human experience. When a man says to God, on the basis of Christ's redemption, "I will;" when he unlocks the door of his heart to admit Christ's gracious presence; a miracle takes place. Dave's life was spring-cleaned of everything unsavoury. Evil habits were dropped and bad language disappeared. He was forgiven into a new relationship with God. He was made a "new creature in Christ." He became a Christian. His life was so consistent that even his furious rebellious wife entered into the same experience, and their little home now radiates the presence of the Master whom they seek to serve with all their hearts.

My friend, you can intellectually convince me that the new motor car you possess is a wonderful vehicle. I can listen to the engine with appreciation of its mechanism and can relax in its upholstery with stirred emotions. It's magnificent. But when I ask you for a ride and you say, "It hasn't a gearbox!"...that's where I get out. As far as I'm concerned its power is useless and its upholstery a waste of material. I can enjoy my fireside armchair a lot better. You see, it is only when the gear-box is in mesh that the car takes me comfortably to my destination.

So it is with God. The gear-box is the will. I can be convinced that God is all powerful, and I can be stirred to the depths emotionally when I hear of the way in which I can rest in Him… but until I do something about it, until I get into gear by saying like Dave, "I will," I don't get any further.

It is the same with marriage. The preacher doesn't say, "Do you believe she will be faithful?" "Do you believe he will provide for your needs?" He says "Will you receive him?" "Will you receive her?"—and the answer comes "I will." That clinches the matter. And when we say the same to God; when we say "I will" to Jesus Christ by opening the door of our heart to His gentle knocking and pulling back the bolt and letting Him into our lives, the same thing happens. We clinch matters with God, and not even death can separate us from Him.

Will you say "I will," right now?

15

After-Shocks

*...that those things which cannot be
shaken may remain. (Hebrews 12:27)*

It was a perfect day. Fiji had never looked better. From the window of our home on the coast about four miles from the city we could see the shimmering coral sea through the waving palms on our front lawn. Pink bougainvillea, smothering the roof of our garage and fanned by the delightfully cool breeze, added to the exquisite nature of the setting. Bunches of orchids were exotically framed against the blue skies and white clouds, raising their magnificent purple heads to nod their appreciation as they were kissed by myriads of dancing dragon flies. The air was filled with the scent of jasmine. We shall never forget the setting.

I took the children into Suva to collect the mail and obtain some commodities for their new term at school which started the next day. We parked outside the post office, and were opening up welcome letters from the homeland, when suddenly I heard what I thought was a tremendous explosion. There was a violent onrush of air and the van shook and trembled with the repercussion.

"On the floor, children," I cried and they instantly obeyed, throwing themselves between the seats. My first reaction was that an ammunition ship had blown up in the harbour, and I awaited the onslaught of debris which I thought would surely rain down upon us. Nothing much more happened, so I peeped through the window to see a most amazing sight. Telegraph posts were waving to each other. Shop windows were falling out of their frames. There was a deadly silence. Then almost instantaneously hundreds of office workers and shop assistants poured out of the buildings into the streets in a dazed condition. Suva had been hit by an earthquake.

We learned, later, that many thought the end of the world had come as typewriters were flung off tables, and some even called to God for help! In a very short while there was pandemonium as taxi drivers sounded their horns in an attempt to get through the crowds, and we decided the best thing to do would be to make for home to see what had happened down the coast.

It was an unforgettable ride. Water surged up and down the creeks and huge cracks appeared in the roadway. A road bridge was severed by gaps at each end and an Indian was frantically signalling me to stop. I could see there was still an opportunity for me to cross the gaps and I took the chance before they widened to prevent me. As we wound our way around the coast we saw an amazing sight. The tide was receding at an enormous rate, just as though a giant hand had pulled a plug out of the harbour bottom, and everything was going out to sea including boats, logs and debris. We stopped to get a better view, and with the ground trembling like jelly under our feet we surveyed the scene. As the tide receded it was also creating an enormous wave which was beginning to tower over the reef, increasing in size every moment. Suddenly this broke and the waters returned with tremendous force to inundate everything in their path, actually crossing the main road and drowning some inhabitants in their homes a few miles away. A fishing party was never seen again. It was a breathtaking sight.

We decided it was time to continue our journey home to find out what had happened there. We discovered the rest of the family on the front lawn, wondering what to do next as the after-shocks were continuing every few seconds. Fijians were beginning to pack their belongings and make for the mountains behind our home. People living in concrete or brick houses refused to go inside. Wooden places were much safer, as they gave under the strain.

The next thing was to listen to the radio and find out what had happened. We soon learned. Apparently the earthquake which had hit Suva had been a severe one of considerable intensity, but although some lives had been lost, the tremor had occurred when the tide was out, and the reef had broken the force of the tidal wave. Had the tide been full, there is no knowing whether I would be alive today to tell the tale, as the city would have been inundated.

We were warned to expect after-shocks for some considerable time, and I believe these were in many ways more alarming than the original earthquake. At first they came at intervals of a few minutes. We could hear the reverberation approaching along the coast, seconds before it hit us. It was quite uncanny. After the shake we could detect the rumble of its disappearance as well. The first ones were quite big, and as nobody knew whether another earthquake was on the way or not, it was a most apprehensive experience. Just as my wife and I were getting into bed that night we heard one approaching and the whole place lifted like a ship on the ocean.

The shocks continued at regular intervals and did not stop for about two years or more. Gradually the frequency altered from once a day to once a week then once a month, and so on. But it took a long time to adjust to the situation, which proved to be a war of nerves for those who had experienced the initial earthquake.

What can we learn from such an unusual experience? Well, first quite a number came to Christ as a result. We know of one woman who was gloriously converted after attending some special meetings we advertised when I spoke on "Earthquake Experiences from the Scriptures." The attendance was amazing. Hundreds of people were really shaken in more ways than one. But as the years rolled by, many forgot that it had ever happened.

I think the most striking lesson can be learned from the after-shocks, for these were the most alarming of all. Coupled as they were with rumours of possible volcanic eruptions, you can imagine the rest. You see, the initial earthquake had been like a soul-shattering experience which takes everybody by surprise and hardly registers. A man goes off with a woman, leaving his wife and family to fend for themselves. It is a dreadful thing, but somehow the initial shock is so great it hardly registers. It is the aftershocks that are so devastating and nerve-shattering. If only people would realise that the outcome of sin is not over in a few minutes, but the repercussions go on indefinitely!

I have recently received a letter from a friend in New Zealand who informed me that a certain prominent individual, who some time ago scandalised a Christian community by an outrageous sin, has now been forgiven and restored to the fellowship of the church, but the shock will still remain. There you have it! I venture to say that although this man may have repented with tears-and I trust he has—the after-shocks of his behaviour will continue for a considerable time. Like the earthquake in Suva, it is not all over in a few seconds. The ground has to adjust itself to the new strata just as this man will have to readjust himself to both the Christian and non-Christian environment to which he belongs. It is a costly business. The repair bills are high. Society, like a city, cannot be shaken without much damage and detriment. It is an alarming thing to suspect that the next after-shock might be the real thing all over again! So it is with the man who has shocked society by his detestable sin. He is viewed with constant suspicion until such a time as the after-shocks subside.

When will man learn that sin never pays? Truly, "the wages of sin is death"... and "the soul that sinneth, it shall die." "Whatsoever a man soweth, that he must reap"—if he sows to the flesh he is bound to reap corruption.

It may be that some who read this are suffering because of the after-shocks of their own sin. Remember, "If we confess our sins, He is faithful and just to forgive us our sins and to cleanse us from all unrighteousness." Yet, it is true we can be restored back to real fellowship with God if we truly repent of our sins and confess them to Him. This is indeed wonderful, but don't expect to be fully restored to society or to some loved one until you have proved through the after-shocks that you can be trusted again. It takes time. Perhaps you are suffering because of the aftershocks of somebody else's sin. This is tough, but remember, if God has forgiven them, who are you to condemn? The heartache, the lack of trust, the after-shock may be great. You have no doubt suffered much, but if you can forgive from the depth of your heart, if you can overcome the fear of the after-shocks which are bound to come from time to time, you are well on the way to a life of great blessing. The answer to earthquake experiences and after-shocks is to be found in Him alone who said, "My peace I give unto you: not as the world giveth, give I unto you. Let not your heart be troubled, neither let it be afraid."

16

Billy Graham

*Thou desirest truth in the
inward parts. (Psalm 51:6)*

Every missionary's experience is high-lighted by important
events in his or her life. Ours has been no exception. In the very
early days of Billy Graham's ministry, the famous evangelist
was known to two of my good friends, Stephen Olford and the
late Joe Blinco. I had often wished to meet Billy, little realising
how prominent his ministry would become as the years rolled
by. Imagine then how I felt when I received a telegram from
Grady Wilson saying that Dr Graham was leaving Honolulu
for the Fiji Islands and would appreciate a welcome at Nadi
airport. There was little time to do much planning, but we
managed to arrange for a car load of Christian friends to
drive over from Suva while we prepared a welcome from the
Lautoka end. It so happened that I was conducting meetings
in that area at the time.

As soon as the plane touched down, we realised what a humble man of God Billy Graham really is! He could have briefly smiled and shaken hands before retiring to the air-conditioned lounge, where a V.I.P. office had been arranged. Instead, he chose to have coffee with us, and chat with the Indian and Fijian young people who had gathered to make him welcome. We took photos of him and Grady Wilson in their shirtsleeves and later he addressed us in an informal manner. Garlanded in typical South Sea fashion with exotic leis he thoroughly enjoyed the occasion and I had the privilege of extending an official welcome on behalf of the churches in Fiji. He was on his way to those first historic Crusades in Australia and New Zealand. His charming, unaffected manner won the hearts of us all, and the way in which he shared a number of questions and problems put to him by our equally unassuming young people was a delight to behold.

A few weeks later another telegram arrived, asking if I would go over to Sydney to share in the blessing of the Crusade. I could hardly believe it. A Christian business man would pay all my expenses, and I would also have a part in the ministry. How fantastic! Surely the Lord makes up to his missionary servants for the cost of leaving all for His sake.

I will never forget those days of fellowship with Bev Shea, Cliff Barrows, Walter Smythe and other members of the team. More often than not, I travelled with Billy to his Crusade meetings, as my host was acting as his chauffeur. Many times I excused myself, not wishing to barge into his privacy, but he always enquired after me. The days were busy visiting schools, colleges and remand homes on behalf of- the team, and the interest in spiritual things was fantastic. I was also given the privilege of bringing a message of greetings from Fiji to the vast crowds at the Sydney showground, an unforgettable experience. When Cliff handed me a huge pile of tape-recordings to be played over the Fiji Broadcast-ing Commission's network upon my return, he said, "Isn't it wonderful to be in the centre of God's will, Bob?" It certainly was and always is!

Those were amazing days. Many hundreds found the Lord, and the first Australian Crusade ranks as one of Billy's most fruitful in every way. Then there came the night when Billy made an announcement which shook me profoundly. He said that there were a number of men eager to help with the follow-up work, and he commended our ministry to the churches in Australia! We had been praying for a wider oppor-tunity, as our children needed to get away from Fiji to extend their education. Here was the open door, totally unsolicited and wonderfully revealed. I felt so humbled, and yet so deeply moved at the thought of such a new sphere of service. Billy made the same announcement in Adelaide, and later I received in writing his recommendation of my ministry to the people 'down under.' How marvellously this was to be vindicated in the years that lay ahead!

But one of the most wonderful moments of my life was when Billy requested me personally to visit his hotel in Adelaide for a chat and a time of prayer concerning our future. Bev was making coffee when I arrived and Billy was stretched out on a divan answering a telephone call from someone in the States who had just rung up to find how things were progressing with the Crusade. We were soon left alone, and I was able to tell Billy something of our experiences and exercise of heart.

"Well, Bob," he answered. "We don't usually invite anyone to associate with our team until we have known them for some time, but we are right behind you in whatever ministry the Lord opens up in the future." The time concluded with a session of prayer as I knelt alone with this man of God to commit our future to the Lord.

Later, my wife and I visited the States and attended the Los Angeles Crusade, when we stayed with Edwin Orr. Billy insisted that I shared the platform, and shortly afterwards I we visited his home in Montreat to enjoy an evening of I fellowship with his family. Other team members, including Bev Shea and his family, had visited us in Fiji, so we returned the visit to his humble little home near Chicago and spent many happy hours together. We thank God for every dedicated member of the Billy Graham team. Our fellowship with them has always been very sweet and wonderful.

There was one thing Billy mentioned in conversation with me and I will pass this on for what it is worth. He said, "Bob, if the Lord leads you to Australia you may have to face up to a certain amount of opposition. You see, in the , States I am a buffer between the ultra-fundamentalists and the modernists. The ultra-fundamentalists cannot tolerate my attitude to the modernists and the modernists cannot tolerate my attitude to the message. You may experience something of this nature."

I understood perfectly. Further objects of Billy's desires were shared with me in confidence, and I know his motives were the purest imaginable. I have the greatest admiration for this dedicated man of God. He was also a prophet! I had a wonderful period of ministry in Australia, speaking in camps, conferences and conventions. Hundreds responded to the gospel message in many places. Unprecedented opportunities for city-wide campaigns opened up throughout this vast continent, but it was not without its measure of opposition, not so much from outsiders, from people who were unconcerned or unconverted, but from certain 'fundamentalists' who objected to a forthright ministry which brought a good deal of sin to light.

Preaching a message which demands repentance is never easy. Refusing to compromise with sin in gospel preaching is never popular. But it brings results. Maybe this is why Dr. Billy

Graham is one of the most successful evangelists this world has ever seen. He refuses to water down his message and we should follow his example. Where there is blessing, there will always be opposition. As it was with the Master, so it will be with His servants! We can learn a lot about Billy's humility. To be correct doctrinally, to hold the right 'evangelical' viewpoints, without possessing the divine life of Christ is, as Paul declares, to be a 'clanging cymbal,' something that doesn't ring true! I believe this is the weakest point in evangelicalism today.

Don't misunderstand me. The so-called ecumenical crowd who clamour for church unity at the expense of evangelical truth will get nowhere spiritually. Their desire is for uniformity, whereas true unity should exist amongst the children of God through faith in our Lord Jesus Christ. However, the evangelical who cannot see beyond his own viewpoint, who is intolerant of others, who does not really contend for the truth, by is contentious over it, who only joins himself to those of his own persuasion, knows little or nothing of the real meaning of the baptism of the Holy Ghost. The Bible says that the truly converted soul has been "baptised by the Holy Spirit into the Body of Christ"—that is, we have already been made one with every true believer, in spite of denominational differences, from the moment of our conversion. No amount of agreement or disagreement over doctrine can make us more or less one than God has declared. How wonderful! When this happens we do not find that we can have heart fellowship with modernists, but we can at least show them the love of God by a right attitude towards them and I believe that (his is the reason why Billy's ministry bears the stamp of God in such a wonderful way.

A man filled with the love of Christ is always tolerant, but a man who may be right doctrinally, without the love of Christ, is most intolerant. If we hold 'correct views' and lack Calvary love we fit into 1 Corinthians 11 most appropriately. Billy has his enemies, and so have we—and they come from the strangest places. We should make sure that we do not become the enemies of Christ by holding tenaciously to evangelical truth at the expense of a life that, lacks the fragrance of His presence, for "by this shall all men know that ye are My disciples, if ye have love for one another." God is not interested in our merely giving mental assent to the truth. As David declared, "Behold, thou desirest truth in the inward parts." This is it! And when the Truth Himself shines through our redeemed humanity, others will take note that we have been with Jesus. May that be said of you and me. Remember to pray for Billy Graham, that the Lord will continue to bless him mightily and keep him true and humble.

17

Making Restitution

*If I have taken anything from any
man by false accusation, I restore
him fourfold. (Luke 19:8)*

I had been preaching for several days at an Aboriginal mission
in Western Australia where I had been staying with the superintendent and his wife. It had been a wonderful occasion. Even
one of the missionaries accepted the Lord! We had organised
special meetings in the town of Norseman and there had been
a good response.

It was also the first occasion I tasted "witchetty grubs," a delicacy to the Aborigines. The only difference is that I inadvertently
swallowed mine whole without biting their heads off first, which
caused great merriment to everyone but me. I concluded that
perhaps they would bore their way through my innards! I even
had thoughts of them mating up down below! My missionary
friends whispered, "It's a good thing. Without their heads they

leave a horrible gooey mess with an indescribable taste in the mouth for some time!" Ignorance is bliss.

It was during the last of the series of meetings that something wonderful happened which caused great rejoicing to all. For some time much prayer had gone up for a young man who was the black sheep of his family. Apparently he was the only one who just would not have anything to do with the Lord. He was present that night, exactly a year to the very day since he had been thrown out of his car at ninety miles an hour and rescued from certain incineration from the exploding wreckage by two Aborigines who were on their way to church. This, in a sense, infuriated him for he hated the Aborigines as he hated everyone else.

For the past year this young man had been under deep conviction. It was impossible to approach him. When I had called at his home a few days earlier, he had gone off to bed. Yet he was present in the church that night. As the meeting proceeded, there was a spirit of deep conviction as the Word of God was preached. During the singing of the last hymn, amongst those who "went forward" to have dealings with God was a brother of this young man who was a Christian, yet who knew there was something needing to be put right in his life. How we thank God for this! (Are you a Christian who needs to put something right with God or your fellow men? You will never realise how important this is until the Lord reveals what a stumbling block it could be to others. "If the light that is in you be darkness, how great is that darkness!") It was because this young Christian was willing to face up to his wrong by getting out of his seat and moving to the front that his brother, deeply convicted of his need of a Saviour, also got out of his seat and stood with him! The atmosphere was electrifying. The impossible had happened. The black sheep had returned to the fold!

I find it hard to described the situation as tears of gratitude were mixed with tears of deep conviction. Yet there was nothing over-emotional about it. Everything was under control. It was just that God had answered the prayers of His people on behalf of a young man who was fast going to the dogs. It is significant to note that, immediately after he had been helped and counselled and had given his heart to Christ, he voluntarily took his cheque book out of his pocket and wrote a generous donation for the mission's work amongst the Aborigines. Truly, "If any man be in Christ Jesus, he is a new creation... old things are passed away and all things become new." Those whom he had once despised and hated, he now loved with the love of God.

I returned home to Melbourne, on the trans-continental train over the Nullarbor plains, with a deep sense of peace in my heart. God had indeed worked in a wonderful way and quite a number had found the Saviour. The super intendent of the mission was a man of God who had won my heart's admiration and he had shared a matter with me that made me realise his worth. Something had happened to one of his daughters which humanly speaking would have driven me away from that area for good, but this had only served to make him more devoted than ever to the people to whom God had called him. He and his wife were a brave devoted couple whose reward will be great. They were untiring in their unswerving dedication to their Lord. He told me how often he pleaded the cause of the Aborigines in court, although he never condoned their wrong-doing. He or his wife were frequently called out of bed at all hours to settle factions in the villages. I take my hat off to them both.

But it was a few days later that the crowning event took place. I received a letter from them to say that the young man who had been so gloriously converted, the man who had been remarkably saved from incineration when his car exploded just a year before, had faced up to something in his new found experience which really proved where he stood before God and his fellow men. True conversion is a very real thing, and this is what happened. Apparently, after the car accident, he had filled out forms to his insurance company and collected the sum of £800 as compensation for the loss of his car. As soon as he became a Christian he realised what a dishonest thing this had been in the sight of God! You see, he had been drunk at the time of the accident. There was only one thing to do. He put up some of his land for sale and with the proceeds sent £800 back to the insurance company, explaining that since he had become a Christian he could no longer make a false claim. The superintendent told me that this act of restitution had resulted in much blessing all around and that the young man was simply rejoicing in his new found faith.

We are living in such shallow days, that it seems to me that in the light of a so-called 'conversion' a man can steal £500 the night before this experience yet keep it afterwards... because everything has been forgiven. This is not God's way out of the situation. Forgiveness does not wipe out a man's debt to his neighbour, although it certainly wipes out his debt to God. Men who have got right with God have gone to prison voluntarily to help pay for debts they could not otherwise discharge. In fact, some dishonest men would readily become so-called Christians if they could thus escape their obligations! Some poor fellow is grinding in jail because he was caught red-handed. Why should another escape because he becomes a Christian? The question of restitution has been left out of the reckoning of many who would find an easy way out. Zacchaeus still says to Jesus, "Behold, Lord, the half of my goods I give to the poor; and if I have taken anything from any man by false accusation, I restore him fourfold."

Just before I left Norseman I was presented with gifts by the local Christians, including a teaspoon for my wife inscribed with the name of the town. This is very precious to us as it holds so many wonderful memories. I think of the vast area of uncultivated bushland, relieved here and there by beautiful salmon gums, their smooth red trunks supporting masses of fragrant olive green leaves. I remember the kangaroos leaping in front of the car as they were attracted by the headlights at night, often a great source of danger to motorists. I think of the beautiful gem-stones for which the area is famous, many of which can be obtained simply by fossicking. But my most cherished memory is of that young man who not only came to Christ, but who gave of his goods to the Aborigines and followed this up by selling part of his land and returning his compensation money to the insurance company. This modern young Zacchaeus knew how wonderfully the Lord came to seek and save that which was lost!

My friend, I wonder if you have to put something right with others before God's blessing can become real in your experience? We are not saved in that way, but when we are saved in God's way, by accepting Christ as our own personal Saviour and Lord, we want to put things right and keep them that way too.

18

Blessed Assurance

*...that ye may know that ye have
eternal life... (1 John 5:13)*

"Do you believe in 'eternal security'?" This question was once asked by an enquirer who sought me out after a challenging message given in a Tasmanian town where a local cinema had been hired for an evangelistic crusade. The place was crowded that night, and a number had professed salvation. Several had actually left the building under deep conviction of sin, but were compelled to return to make peace with God.

My subject that night had been one which I rarely touch upon... the flames of Hell. I had returned to my host's home, and was about to get into bed, when there was a knock at the door. "Someone wants to see you..." was the answer to my query.

I donned my dressing gown and went into the lounge, to meet a young man obviously looking very troubled indeed.

"I feel the flames of Hell licking after me," was the reason given for his intrusion. This encouraged me. Not many enquirers these days come for help and advice on that level. My preaching must have gone home. Praise God for such a deep conviction!

As we sat down together seeking God's mind, he suddenly looked in my direction and said, "Mr. Stokes, do you believe in 'eternal security'…?" This took me completely by surprise. A person who feels the flames of Hell licking after him rarely asks such a question. My suspicions were immediately aroused. What was the object of this visit? What did he know about such Christian teachings anyway? How could I answer his question? I was careful in my reply. "If you mean by 'eternal, security' that a person who is truly converted will never be lost, I wholeheartedly believe in the teaching… but this needs to be clarified. Anyway, why is it that you, who feel the flames of Hell licking after you, should want to ask such a question? Are you not more concerned with your soul's salvation than what happens to the Christian? Why do you come here at this late hour, to ask something that concerns someone who no longer fears the flames of Hell?"

He then told me that some time back he had "made a decision for Christ", had gone on well for a short while but was now troubled about his soul's salvation. Could I give him any hope that he was on his way to Heaven? My answer was definite. Only the Holy Spirit could give the assurance he now needed. Seeing that he felt the flames of Hell licking after him, he could hardly be a converted man, but who was I to assure him, even through the Word of God, that he was on his way to Heaven? Did he have the witness of the Spirit that he was a child of God? If not, why not?

I then suggested that we got down to prayer together, but was again suspicious of the circumstances surrounding his life because he just could not pray! Something was desperately wrong. A man who was troubled about his soul's salvation, in spite of the fact that at some time or other he had made a decision for Christ, was unable to pray in my presence. There was only one thing to do—to challenge him about his manner of living. He was soon out with it. I was astounded. He told me that he had left his wife and was living with another woman, yet he wanted me to give him the assurance that he was on his way to Heaven, while he was living in sin!

This is the tragedy of 'decisionism' or a cheap and easy 'believism.' I am sure there are thousands of those who claim to be evangelical Christians who have never been 'born again.' They may have given mental assent to the truth in some evangelistic campaign, possibly because they did feel the flames of Hell licking after them, but there was no deep conviction of sin resulting in true repentance of heart and life. Theirs was an escapist policy at Christ's expense. This is the great danger of signing decision cards, or raising one's hand in response to the evangelist's appeal, without a deep realisation of the nature of sin. When this is followed by Christian baptism, a place at the Lord's Table, and a share in the fellowship of the local church, the result is disastrous. It is even worse when the teaching of 'eternal security' follows!

It is perfectly true that no Christian is sinless. "If we say we have no sin we deceive ourselves, and the truth is not in us." It is also wonderfully true that "If we confess our sins, He is faithful and just to forgive us our sins..." but it does not stop there. Listen to this, *"and to cleanse us from all unrighteousness!"* The born again Christian knows that his sin will not prevent him from going to Heaven, but he is miserable until he gets right with God.

This is the position of the backslider. We must not confuse backsliding with never having been born again. There is a great difference. The backslider is miserable in his sin, and deep down inside longs to get right with God, although he may put up a fight against repentance for some time. The so-called 'decisionist' could not care less about his sin provided he can also hold on to the truth of eternal security, which is- more important to him than repentance. Those who confess their sins to the Lord with the desire to be done with their sin are entirely different from those who merely confess with the object of securing their salvation at the same time!

I lost no time in telling the young man that not even God could give him the assurance of his salvation under such circumstances. Here is someone who feels the flames of Hell licking after him; who wants me to give him an assurance from God's Word that he is going to Heaven while he is living in sin. The nearest approach to the truth was obvious. He was feeling the flames of Hell, because he had never been converted. His so-called 'decision' just was not conversion.

But did I leave him there? Did I want to see him consumed in the flames of Hell? Not on your life! Now was the time for God to work. This was the opportunity for the evangelist. I then said something like this. "Young man, you can know freedom from this terrible haunting fear of torment in Hell. You can know what it is like to have a real assurance that your sins are forgiven, and that you are on your way to Heaven. Get on your knees and confess your sin to God, putting this woman out of your life right now, and going back to your wife if she will have you... there is no other way. The Lord will then forgive you and also cleanse you from all unrighteousness."

He hesitated for some time, and then, slowly rising from his chair, he lamely said, "Goodnight, Mr. Stokes. I will pray about it," and sadly went out into the darkness of that night, with the flames of Hell still licking after him because tit was true. He was not willing to have done with his sin, yet he wanted to go to Heaven, an absolute impossibility. It was not so much that his sin was damning him, it was his unwillingness to forsake it, to be done with it—and that is the proof that a man has never come face to face with Jesus Christ.

I believe that those who start with God on the basis of repentance and faith, when they come to Christ will go on with God, whether whole-heartedly or half-heartedly. There will be a growth to some degree. There will be evidence. There will be a hatred of sin and a love for Christ. But 'decisionists' are different, they will even cling to the Scriptures for their own benefit, irrespective of their Sinful manner of living. It must be agonising to the true Christian not to know for certain that he is saved, but I would sooner meet the man who loves the Lord yet has doubts concerning his security than someone living in sin who is cocksure about his salvation.

You see, I believe in the precious truth of 'eternal security,' but I do not advocate teaching this truth to 'decisionists' who have never been truly born again. After all, this blessed assurance is conveyed to the heart, not the intellect, by the Holy Spirit, whose purpose it is to keep the believer true to the Lord Jesus Christ, and such assurance is never associated with unholy living. It is a wonderful thing to be able to say, "Blessed assurance, Jesus is mine"—for time and for eternity! Can you say that with me?

The years have rolled by... and with great joy we can tell you that this man has repented, sought Christ's forgiveness, and now knows the truth of eternal security.

19

Wedding Catastrophe

*Now we see through a glass darkly; but
then face to face. (1 Corinthians 13:12)*

At last the day had dawned for the wedding of our daughter, Gillian. It was a beautiful morning and all the plans had worked out remarkably well Gillian had met her beloved some years before at a Youth for Christ houseparty on the Dandenong Hills above Melbourne, when her father was the guest speaker. We all grew very fond of Warren and he had come into great spiritual blessing as a result of his friendship with Gillian. Moreover we were to be united to a lovely Christian family, as Warren's father was an evangelical Baptist minister who had spent a number of years with his wife and family as a missionary in Africa. We had watched our daughter's friendship with great interest and rejoiced when Warren asked for her hand in marriage. They both had plans for Bible training, although both had been employed in secular occupations up to now. They had our blessing on this very happy occasion. Little did we think what the day would hold for us all, apart from the wedding. We rose early knowing that so much depended on a successful start, especially as her two sisters would be brides-maids. But there was something I wanted to do before the ceremony—something which might make all the difference at the reception from the photogenic point of view. I had noticed that the bridal party would be seated in front of a modern brick wall which to my mind was hardly the background for a photograph when the cake was cut. It needed a good long set of curtains to hide the bricks. A friend of ours was willing to take her lovely drapes down and lend them to us for the occasion. In fact, she would come along with me. In due course we were proceeding down the road with long curtain rods jutting out of the car windows, making for the place of the reception.

It was not going to be an easy job to erect these curtains. Windows high up in the brick wall were at least ten feet from the ground and provided the only vantage point. What was needed was a good long ladder. We managed to find the largest and longest step-ladder I have ever seen in my life, no doubt specially designed for dealing with these windows.

It was here that I made my big mistake. Instead of using it as a step-ladder, I propped it in a folded position against the wall to give extra height, and proceeded to the top. I had been up twice and there remained the third and last curtain to fix. Standing on the top rung adjusting the curtain, I felt the ladder slip and in a few terrifying seconds I had crashed to the ground, smashing part of the ladder on the way. Something snapped in my shoulder and I thought I had also broken my leg. I lay in agony on the ground. My daughter's wedding was two hours away, and here was I helpless and in great pain. Oh, why should such a thing happen at such a time as this?

A Baptist minister who happened to live nearby was on the spot in a few minutes and as I nursed my shoulder we shared together some precious thoughts concerning the sufferings of our Lord. I have always found such times conducive to remembering His agony in a very real way. A doctor had been sent for, someone unknown to me, but who lived close by. After a few minutes' examination he gave me an injection and then rolled up his sleeves to twist the arm back into its socket, as he reckoned I was only suffering a dislocation. His diagnosis was wrong, and instead of getting the arm back where it should have been, he pulled four broken pieces of bone out of the socket and plunged them into the muscle bed instead!

By this time I was reeling from shock and pain and in this condition I was sent back home to prepare for the wedding. Nauseated beyond words, I was violently sick and naturally turned up to give Gillian away looking "like death warmed up" as someone put it. It was as much as I could do to sit through the ceremony, and after a rest, to attend at least part of the reception; but as I committed my way to the Lord I was enabled to make my speech without experiencing any pain whatever, and then immediately left for the X-ray department. But it was a simply wonderful wedding. Christ was exalted throughout and even the loving sympathy of many of our Christian guests seemed to enhance the occasion.

That evening Melbourne's top specialist was in our home trying to explain to me that he had never seen a bigger mess than my smashed shoulder. I was to be operated on the next morning, Sunday, and the biggest problem was getting the broken pieces of bone out of the muscle before attempting to piece them together in the socket! We had a word of prayer in the operating theatre and the Lord honoured this in many wonderful ways. The surgeon took two hours to do the job. When I was coming round he whispered in my ear such comforting words—he said, "You are going to experience a lot of pain."

What a prophet he turned out to be! For days, for weeks and even months my shoulder ached and ached and ached. There was always the possibility of damage to blood cells during those first twenty-four hours when the broken bones lay in the muscle bed, and also the risk of infection during the operation. I had been told quite frankly that my left arm would never be normal again—that its use would be limited and I would never be able to paint the ceiling with it or anything like that! There is always the question "Why?"—and as I lay on my bed tossing and turning, I would occasionally wonder why this was allowed to happen. One day when the pain was very acute, someone left a gift of £100 towards expenses in a letter which was dropped in our letterbox. Who knows but that this exercise of heart might never have taken place apart from the accident?

It was a slow process towards recovery-and I almost cried with despair as I failed to make use of the arm for such a long time. Then I discovered a wonderful means of therapy. On our way by sea from Australia to England a few months later, I found I could use breast stroke in the swimming pool, and day after day I perservered until the arm miraculously eased up and began to function again. A doctor friend told me that this was probably the best possible means of recovery. After a little more than two years, I found that I could paint the ceiling with my left hand—in fact, nobody would know now, apart from an enormous scar, that there has ever been anything wrong with it.

But what has come out of it all to glorify Christ? That is the big question we have a right to ask at all times. Was I a witness to those preparing the wedding breakfast as I lay in agony on the ground after the accident? Was I a witness as I took my place at the wedding service and later made my speech at the reception? Was I a witness to the medical profession at the hospital? Was I a witness during those difficult days of convalescence? Was I a witness as I struggled through the therapeutic treatment? Was I a witness to my own family throughout? There must have been a wise purpose behind it all, and although we cannot see things very clearly from this end, God knows that from His standpoint this broken shoulder is one of the "all things" that "work together for good to them that love the Lord, who are called according to His purpose."

One day we shall know for certain why I fell headlong from the top of that ladder, quite apart from my own stupidity in not seeing that it was securely fastened. In any case one of these purposes might be the telling of this story to you now to encourage you in your dilemma to trust the Lord! The Baptist minister who shared some of those precious thoughts concerning the Lord's sufferings as I lay waiting for the doctor to arrive, brought this experience into his sermon the following Sunday morning when it was a blessing to quite a few people—so we little know just what can come out of an accident of this nature. There is much, of course, that we shall never be able to understand down here—"now we see through a glass darkly, but then face to face."

20

An Inferiority Complex

*If we confess our sins, He is faithful and
just to forgive us our sins. (1 John 1:9)*

I had just experienced a wonderful time of blessing on the
mission field. Special meetings had been arranged for the
encouragement of the missionaries and I had been asked to
bring the messages. In fact, an invitation was given to me
to extend my itinerary to certain areas in the United States,
where this type of ministry was so much needed. One of the
missionaries had approached me and confessed that there were
certain things in his life which needed to be cleared up, and
the outcome of getting right with God would be nothing
short of explosive in its reactions elsewhere. We thanked the
Lord together for His gracious unveiling of the truth which
had been so dynamic in its outreach.

I was now leaving for meetings in another country and was
awaiting transport to the airport. In the interim I was enjoying

a cup of tea with the wife of one of the senior missionaries, while her little daughter was drinking a glass of milk nearby. There was nobody else to interrupt the conversation.

Turning to me she suddenly said, "Mr. Stokes, before you leave I want to share an experience with you and tell you something that I have never shared with anyone else, not even my husband."

I looked into the face of this attractive young woman, wondering what her story would contain. There was a light about her features, and I recognised that the Lord was having wonderful dealings with her. This was the story she related as we shared that 'cuppa' together. I will try and repeat it as near as my memory will allow, just as she told it to me.

She said, "Years ago, when at college, I had an inferiority complex which I found difficult to deal with, and consequently I was never the centre of attention like some other girls I knew. I was jealous of them and longed to be like them, but how was this .possible? I then hit upon an ingenious little plan. I would make myself the centre of attraction if I could not otherwise manage it. Consequently, whenever a crowd of us were together in the lectures, I would have a convenient little fainting fit, only to find myself the very centre of attention without any trouble at all.

"Mr. Stokes, it worked! I would cross a busy thoroughfare and one of these little 'turns' would immediately bring a crowd of sympathetic folk around me. All I got at the best of times were a couple of bruised knees, but it was well worth it. My little world was satisfied. I would hear everyone talking about me as they lifted me up and tried to revive me. Sometimes I had to bite my lips to stifle an irrepressible laugh as the humour of the situation gripped me!

"This went on for some time until at last my parents became alarmed and arranged for a medical examination to find the cause of these fainting spells. I was examined by a number of specialists who declared that the whole thing might be due to a grumbling appendix. It was, therefore, arranged that I should go into hospital for its removal. They took it out and said that during the operation they had noticed some disarrangement which might possibly be the cause of the blackouts. This they had rectified and there should be no more problems. Well, I determined there would be no more trouble and to the relief of everyone concerned, the fainting fits stopped. It was attributed to the medical skill of the diagnosticians and surgeons but, of course, I knew better!"

She then paused before continuing. "Mr. Stokes, some time ago I read your little book, *A Call to Repentance,* but it left me cold. I have since read it again and there is a story about a young man who knew no peace until he owned up to his mother that he was a liar. That's me, Mr. Stokes. I am the leading missionary's wife, but my Bible has been a dead book for years. I have been assuming a dedication that is not real. For years I deceived my parents into thinking that I was suffering a malady, until at last they paid the heavy expense of an operation to remedy matters. I have had no real peace until now, but as I speak with you my heart knows a new experience of joy... something I have never had for years. You see, I have sorted out this matter before the Lord and He has forgiven me. I am going to write to my parents and tell them the whole business, asking their forgiveness. I am also going to tell my husband everything when you have gone!"

It was an astounding story, and as I looked at this radiant young woman whose little daughter was drinking her milk, all too oblivious of the implications of her mother's candid confession, I just thanked the Lord for the wonder of His amazing grace. She was quite obviously an attractive woman, but now much more so in the light of God's dealings with her in such a wonderful way. I have discovered that when anyone has dealings with God and responds to His claims there is a resultant radiance which is quite unique. It seems that the Spirit of God shines through! Here was someone who had hidden a sin in her heart for years until the Holy Spirit put His finger on the spot and she was willing to make an open confession in order to put things right before the Lord and before those whom she had wronged. Here she was, telling the Lord's servant, whose ministry had opened up the whole situation and brought the issue to light, something which made her redeemed humanity glow with divine pleasure.

I met her again a few years later, and believe me the glow is still there. She has met the Lord in a real way and He has done something wonderful in her life. She faced up to an implication of hypocrisy and unreality in her life which is now cleansed and forgiven as she confessed her wrong. She will never cease to praise God for the resultant peace and joy which is hers. As I shook her hand in a farewell greeting before leaving for the airport, I thanked the Lord for the privilege of being used of Him to plumb the depths of a missionary's strange experience as He brought her back to Himself in such a wonderful way.

Many people are seeking a new experience of the Lord in these bewildering days, but unfortunately a good number of them are looking for something in the realm of their feelings. I am convinced that what is needed is a keener perception of what the Holy Spirit is after in our lives! If there remains any unchecked, unforgiven and unconfessed sin in the heart, there will never be any realisation of God's power, in spite of the fact that some might be able to enter into all kinds of strange experiences. One moment's obedience to the known will of God brings us into the fulness of the blessing.

There is no need to shout to God like some people do for a special kind of blessing. He is not deaf. "His ear is not heavy that it cannot hear," for He knows everything about us before we even tell Him. I am sure He is not terribly impressed when we work ourselves up emotionally. I am certainly not against a few hearty 'Amens' here and there, but remember, there is just as much bondage in repeating it in the wrong place as there is in being silent. If only we would realise that "obedience is better than sacrifice"—better than the sacrifice of time and energy and sweat and blood and tears. Remember, "The Holy Spirit is given to them that *obey* Him." We can get wrapped up in all kinds of wonderful experiences yet fail to obey the Lord. I was in a meeting the other day when a man kept interjecting with a few "Hallelujahs," yet he was one who came forward for counselling. He admitted that he was difficult to live with, always flew off the handle with his wife and never read his Bible. There was no radiance about his countenance or any joy in his experience. He needed to get right with God. Yet he was the very one who repeatedly shouted "Hallelujah!"

Maybe the story of this young lady who said she assumed a kind of dedication because she was the leading missionary's wife is true of you as well. Your mind can fully absorb higher life teaching and you can readily subscribe to sound doctrine, but you are really spiritually dead. Is it possible that you need to obey the Lord somewhere along the line... you need to say "sorry" to someone, to admit that you have done an injury or a wrong? Your self-centred life may seem satisfied, but there is something dreadfully missing. If so, there is only one thing to do, and that is obey the slightest whisper of His Holy Spirit. Get tuned in to the right wave-length now and He will transmit His message to you as He did to this young lady who had to write to her parents and share the matter with her husband. You will then know the radiance of a life in tune with God.

21

Mother's Booby Trap

*Blessed is he,, whosoever shall not be
offended in Me. (Matthew 11:6)*

A while ago I met my mother at Paddington Station and
brought her on to our home in Surrey. It was a long- awaited
visit, held up by a flu epidemic and the very cold weather, so
we had the house beautifully warm for her reception. At eighty-
four years of age, she is small and wizened by the encroaching
erosion of time, yet amazingly agile and active. It is always
wonderful to have her with us. She has been a widow for many
years, yet rejoices in her Lord and Saviour. In many ways she is
a very extraordinary little woman, with certain striking characteristics; and of course she is very much loved by her family.
Let me tell you something that happened to her recently.

Mother is very fond of gardening, and because help is so
difficult to obtain, she does most of the hard work herself.
Many a strong muscular individual would blush to see her

wielding a hefty spade, or pushing a lawn mower. She gets amazing results too! Runner beans are a speciality and she has often given her family a steaming bowl of tender shoots garnished with melted butter for supper... simply delicious! As for her flower beds, they are the envy of the neighbours who wish they had green fingers such as mother has. Naturally she takes a certain amount of keen pride in her garden, but something occurred last year to really hurt this pride.

At the bottom of the garden is a small glasshouse, adjacent to a low lying wall overlooking a green meadow. It is quite-easy for someone to slip over the wall from the outside without being detected. Mother has discovered that the greenhouse is an excellent place for growing really luscious tomatoes. Her crop excelled itself, and fine ripe fruit was the outcome of her labours. Someone else discovered this by prying over the wall one night, and the next morning all the best tomatoes had gone. How galling it was for Mother to find that, instead of being able to give some of her fruit to her friends and neighbours, a thief had gone off with the best of the pick!

This happened so many times, that at last out of sheer exasperation Mother hit on a brilliant plan. Surely if the thief could not be caught, he must at least suffer a rude lesson for his wickedness. Mother accordingly got out her spade and dug a nice deep pit just inside the greenhouse door right across the pathway inside. When the hole was big enough to catch its victim, she filled it up with thick slimy mud. She chuckled to think of the intruder's dilemma when he stumbled into her neat little trap!

A few days later there was a great cry, as the victim fell headlong into the sticky mess... but alas, it was not the unwelcome intruder. It was Mother, who had completely forgotten about her little plan! She is so small, that the hole well and truly enveloped her and she emerged a frightful sight, smothered from head to foot in the mud she had so carefully prepared for the thief! If her pride had been truly hit by the theft, surely there was not much of it left by now.

But that was not all. Sometime later my brother, who lives nearby, asked Mother how the trap was faring. Had the thief been caught? Was there evidence that he had met his match in Mother's carefully prepared plan? Mother paused for a moment before replying, and then she said in her own characteristic way, causing my brother to rock with laughter, "Well if you want to know, I've gone and done it again…!" For the second time she had fallen a victim to her own trap, and this time bruised her legs into the bargain.

When I heard the story, knowing my mother as I do, I too was convulsed with laughter. I can see her pained look, and vividly imagine the whole situation as she tumbled headlong into the gooey mess for the second time. Maybe there was a measure of compensation later on when she discovered evidence that the thief too had met with the same misfortune on one of his nightly rounds! At any rate it seemed at least to stop the loss of the tomatoes.

This little human story about my dear mother contains many lessons. In the first place, if we are Christians—and I trust that you have received the Lord Jesus Christ into your heart, for there is no other way to become a Christian—then we are going to meet with a lot of disappointments in life. There will be corners of our vineyard of which we shall be rightly proud. There will be a sense of achievement in all that is done in Christ's name. Our little garden will no doubt bear fruit as a result of our witness, our testimony and our ministry. We will have worked hard for the produce. Souls will have found the Saviour, and there will be a sense of satisfaction in knowing that God has given the increase to the sowing and watering of His Word.

We must remember however, that there is a thief abroad who desires to remove the fruit for himself. He comes in the dead of night, when we are unaware of his presence, 'and before we realise it, he has robbed us of the first fruits of our labours in the service of the Master. This happens constantly. The servants of God will be tested. There will come a time when it seems that we have laboured for many weary years... all for nothing. Someone else takes the credit for what we have done, because the thief has robbed ,us of the evidence of our labours by taking the best of the fruit! It took us years to know how to sow, before we started to learn the art of reaping. Then God gave us the increase, and we rejoiced in a wonderful harvest. All of a sudden there was nothing to show for it. Just when the evidence was needed to justify our wholehearted devotion to Christ in sheer hard work with little or no reward, the thief came along and robbed us of the fruit. Our pride was sorely hit. A novice reaped the reward instead. We were not chosen for that conference. We were left out of the reckoning of the board members. We were overlooked in the decision for a delegate. Our garden, once the envy of onlookers, was stripped by the Enemy and showed nothing but barrenness instead. It was hard to take. In fact rumours had spread that seeing there was no fruit in evidence, there possibly never had been any anyway...! We knew an Enemy had been busy, but perhaps the rumour-mongers did not. It made it even harder to take. Our pride was wounded and hurt beyond measure. Some have even turned away from the Lord because of these things. Whenever I am tempted to do so, I think of His own words: "Blessed is he, whosoever shall not be offended in Me..."

We may have thought of a scheme, like my mother's, to trap the Enemy. We planned a carefully thought out strategy which took considerable painstaking time and energy in prayer letters, committee meetings, and visitation, only to fall into disrepute ourselves and to make things ten times worse! The mud we had planned for someone else stuck to us instead. We learned that the ways of the Lord are not our ways. Eventually, because we were willing to humble ourselves and confess our wrong doing in seeking to rectify matters, something we had never forseen in our busy sowing and reaping, the Lord brought us into a wealthy place of real blessing, and the Enemy ceased from his tactics!

What we learn from the humorous incident of my little mother and her mud bath is that there is "a time for every purpose" as the Scriptures declare. Not only a time to be born, and a time to die... but a time to be humbled as well as to be exalted. A time to be quiet, as well as to be busy. A time to be tested as well as to be praised. A time to be forgotten as well as to be remembered. If we can go through these times without being offended, we will truly be called blessed.

John the Baptist's ministry ended in seclusion and solitary confinement before he was beheaded. Certainly the Enemy stripped him of his fruitful calling and he questioned, even as we do, the wisdom of it all! It was to him in particular as well as to us in general, that the Lord said, "Blessed is he, whosoever shall not be offended in Me." Mother's experience reminds us of Psalm 7 verse 15: "He made a pit and digged it, and is fallen into the ditch which he made!" Let us be careful that we do not fall into such a trap.

22

The Driving Test

*I will guide thee with
mine eye. (Psalm 32:8)*

A veteran driver for over thirty-five years, I have just passed my driving test! It was quite an experience. You see, my previous British licence was over ten years old, and I had been driving with an Australian one backed by an international licence which is valid until one takes up permanent residence in this country. I was able to continue in this way because of my many travels overseas in the meanwhile.

It is surprising how one's driving habits become so much a part of one, and I decided to take up a few lessons to rectify many of mine. My first lesson almost drove me to despair! Looking over your shoulder as well as viewing in the mirror; changing down to second and using the handbrake at the lights; holding the steering wheel a certain way; looking right, left, and right again at intersections; hand signals when passing stationary vehicles; making sure your foot is not on the clutch when cornering, which cuts out a fast change; all these, and more besides, made me wonder if I would ever pass the test!

Oh yes, I am a careful driver, with virtually no accidents to my debit, but how easy to form one's own habits of driving! My instructor informed me that the Highway Code was designed for better driving, so I hope it has done me some good, but I wonder how many, like myself, will possibly lapse into old ways after a while? I reckon it is far easier for a beginner, taking lessons for the very first time, to pass the test than for a seasoned driver with formed habits to get through. I am glad I only needed one test to comply with the regulations, for the family were convinced that I would fail! For once they were wrong. Dad exceeded all expectations!

Firstly, starting off on a trip. I was always careful about this, making sure by looking in the mirror that the way was perfectly clear in all directions; but I had never thought of looking over my shoulder as well. Perhaps we could call this the "backward look." It's certainly a safe procedure, and Paul recommends it every time we desire to make a fresh start. Looking back over the past for a few brief moments will ensure us that we do not make the same mistakes, or that these mistakes will not overtake us again. We must not assume that the road is clear until we are certain about these things.

We can all learn a lot from past experiences. History need not repeat itself. Sins and shortcomings need not crowd into the highway and impede our progress. And Paul says that when the road is clear, we can readily forget those things which are behind, and press on towards the mark for the prize of the high calling of God in Christ Jesus. This gives us a very good start. The Highway Code says nothing about glancing over one's shoulder at any other time! We must then keep our eyes ahead, looking for all the hazards of the new trip and obeying all the signals. This secures safety, certainty and enjoyment on the road of life.

Then we must make sure the signal is given before we move forward. This is very important. We can get very careless about this at times. We all know the danger resulting from drivers who move out into the highway without signalling their intentions. The code says: "Mirror, signal and then manoeuvre." As a Christian I must signal my intentions at all times. If not, then I will get caught up in the traffic of life and be in danger of a collision course. I must signal my intentions in the office that I have nothing to do with gambling, otherwise my money will go on the next sweepstake instead of being used to support the Lord's people. I must signal my intentions to turn away from doubtful conversations, otherwise I will laugh with them at the next dirty joke. I must signal my intentions to keep clear from drink and drugs, otherwise I will compromise at the next Christmas party. Looking in the mirror to see what is coming up always prepares us for good signaling, and once we have made ourselves clear, then the way is open for a fresh manoeuvre. Our driving habits are being scrutinized carefully, and if we are careful Christians, making good signals whenever necessary, our presence on the highway of life will be appreciated by all. This opens up the way for manoeuvring the situation in a skilful way, leading men and women to the cross-roads of decision, and showing them the highway to life abundant and life eternal. Example is better than precept. They will follow us if we are good drivers.

Next the traffic lights. We must never proceed against the red light of warning, but slow down and come to a gradual halt. This does not mean that our Christian lives are brought to a standstill. On the contrary, we slip into second gear ready to move away as soon as the way is clear. I like that! Danger signs abound on the Christian highway, and there are times when we must stop dead in our tracks to avoid a catastrophe. We have an inbuilt traffic system which tells us when to slow down, stop dead or proceed. There is always danger ahead. Today these dangers abound as never before—the danger of compromise, the danger of worldliness, the danger of evangelical hardness, the danger of immorality, the danger of cold-heartedness, the danger of materialism, and many other dangers besides.

Our conscience, enlightened by the Holy Spirit, gives us the red light of warning, the yellow light of caution, and the green light of continuance. The Christian never stops at the red light longer than is necessary. He is ready for the positive sign of moving ahead in the will of God. The road also abounds with yellow, lights of caution. We must be careful not to run people down. Perhaps this is one of the most dangerous practices of all. People are crossing our pathway every moment of the day, and we must see that we give them due recognition and reverence. They have traffic rights as well as we do. If we slow down well in advance, and respect the caution sign, we will not get involved in incidents and accidents. To smash a man's reputation to pieces by disobeying the signals is far worse than afflicting him physically. Running people down by carelessness and recklessness is something from which they may never fully recover.

Watch out for the caution signs. They will flash ominously in good time, but remember your journey will always be made most reassuring and relaxing when the green lights are showing. You don't have to look to the right hand or to the left under such circumstances, but keep straight on. Even in the most congested areas, with traffic on all sides, you can always be sure of the safety of the green light. The Christian can forge ahead only when the road is clear!

Then the hazards. Perhaps the most dangerous of all is overtaking. If the way is not clear, how foolish to try to overtake. It is often impossible to see around a bend, or over a hill, or through a thick fog, yet many risk their own lives as well as those of others by attempting to pass in spite of these conditions. The Bible is clear about overtaking. It says, "If a man be overtaken by a fault, let him that is spiritual restore such a one in the spirit of meekness, lest he also be tempted." The danger is obvious. We can all criticise and condemn the roadhog, but that will not rectify his driving manners. He may smash himself and involve others as well, but until he learns some road sense and drives with caution, he will always be a menace. How can we approach such a person? I suppose all of us are guilty of breaking the speed limit, so what can we say? The only one who has a right to approach him is the man who, having broken the law, has acquired new driving habits as a result. His experience, even at the cost of a fatal accident, will accomplish more than any amount of advice from one who has never been guilty of any traffic offence. So it is with the Christian. The only one who can help those who have been overtaken by a fault, is the one whose faults have been fully and adequately taken care of by the good Judge of all who doeth right, when He sent His Son, Jesus Christ, into the world to die upon Calvary's cross for our sins.

Cornering too fast on a wet road is another great hazard which calls for much care and attention. Someone has said, "I would sooner get there ten minutes late than to arrive dead on time." Food for thought! Some Christians skid into Heaven before God's time because they have paid little attention to the weather conditions. Fog, snow and ice all call for added care and attention. Changeable spiritual climates are commonplace. We must know how to tackle these situations by the careful study of God's Word, His Highway Code.

Finally, the many road signs symbolised by pictures and lessons have to be carefully studied. My examiner asked me the meaning of these as he drew out his road book and pointed them out one by one. It is a fascinating study. The Word of God is also our infallible guide through life, and its many signs and symbols can only be interpreted by the Holy Spirit as we seek His guidance. There are times when we must not stop, and other times when to stop is imperative. May our driving habits on the Highway of Life be free from carelessness and distraction as we draw nearer and nearer to the Heavenly City.

23

Permissive Society

*...that every mouth may be stopped,
and all the world may become guilty
before God. (Romans 3:19)*

The other night I could not sleep. I admit this is not unusual these days, as a recent X-ray has revealed some spinal trouble, but that night's restlessness was not caused by anything physical. I was in an agony of soul over something I had read in the press which not only nauseated me, but constitutes a great cause for alarm. It concerned the permissive society which is gaining momentum all around us.

You have no doubt all read about the film, *Growing Up,* which has been released, including not only shots of nudity and intercourse, but sinking so low as to reveal close-ups of masturbation by both sexes. My spirit has been outraged by the desire on the part of those responsible to show this film to school children! Some time ago an attempt was made to introduce to our schools a little red book inciting our children not only to sexual perversion, but also to anarchy as well. It seems incredible, almost unbelievable, that our society has sunk so low, but I read in the paper that hundreds of letters have been pouring into Westminster, requesting that something be done about this increase in pornography.

Watching a television interview, I became aware of one of the reasons behind this scandalous desire to pervert the rising generation, and that is to get rid of the guilt problem created by social standards of the past which are no longer acceptable to the modern generation. It seems to me that in an attempt to remove a sense of guilt, our society is declaring war on God Himself, and thereby setting up substandards, allowing the grossest of sins which are being defined as normal healthy habits! It is this question of guilt which concerns me just now. Looked at from God's standpoint, guilt is not as unhealthy as man would have us believe, because it is actually the basis for the solution of the problem in the provision of a Saviour. I believe that the modern permissive society has come into its own because the Church of Jesus Christ has failed to witness to His saving grace and power. It is an indictment of us for our failure to set up Scriptural standards which can be read of all men. May the Lord forgive us. Our Christian lives have failed to produce a sense of guilt in others.

First of all we must clarify the situation by declaring God's standards in the moral realm of sex relationships. These are unchangeable, and there are no exceptions. A generation or two ago the hush-hush policy relating to sex matters did more harm than good, and ignorance concerning the physical outcome of self-indulgence frightened people into thinking they might become insane. However, the pendulum has swung so far in the opposite direction that whereas those guilty of these sins in times past at least tried to overcome them, the hour has now come to indulge in them. We are told that they actually benefit us! I want to declare God's standards in these realms of sex behaviour and then show how the guilt problem can be dealt with as a result.

Masturbation, or having sex on one's own, is certainly wrong and sinful. It is rarely indulged in without associating the habit with thoughts that are dishonouring to God and the opposite sex, which is the most harmful side of the practice. It may not debilitate physically, at least not on the alarming scale suggested in the past, but it is bound to wreck moral and spiritual aspirations. In childhood the habit may be formed accidentally, and wise handling on the part of parents is well rewarded. It is just as wrong as greed or gluttony, and all children are guilty of these abnormalities at some time or another. Its danger may not lie so much in the guilt it produces, as in the terrible power it wields over its victims. Our permissive society wants to get rid of the guilt by suggesting it is not wrong, and deal with its grip by allowing its victims to have casual relationships with the opposite sex. Today you can indulge at will on your own or with others, and thus you are not shut up with the problem as in the past! Consequently children must be taught from childhood or adolesence that not only self-expression is right, but sex-expression as well!

How different from God's way of deliverance! In a Christian home, all sin produces a guilt complex, and there is absolutely nothing wrong with this. Children become guilty over lying, stealing, cheating, disobedience and deceit, in order that they might eventually come to Christ. I would venture to say that thousands of people have become guilty over sex sins in like manner, and as a result have found the Saviour. Nobody will ever enter into the Kingdom of Heaven until they come to Christ as lost, guilty, sinners. It is true that an overwhelming sense of guilt, without a knowledge of the way of deliverance, occasionally leads to psychiatric problems, but these are nothing compared to the moral chaos resulting from uninhibited lives of self-expression in the form of venereal disease, abortions, drug addiction and marriage break-downs. With the advent of the pill all moral restraint has broken down, and we are on the verge of something so appalling that it frightens the most serious minded among us.

Fornication, or sex involving unmarried people, is expressly forbidden by the early church, and can never be right, even during an engagement. This is seen clearly in the possible event of the death of an unmarried father who leaves his child out of wedlock to be brought up by a single girl. We shall soon be hearing of an attempt to abolish marriage in order to be rid of any guilt problem in this direction as well! Adultery, or sex involving unfaithfulness in marriage, is clearly defined to be wrong, and needs no comment. The perversions of sex including homosexuality and bestiality are all outside of the Christian way of life, and are condemned in the Scriptures in no uncertain terms.

This brings me to the question of guilt. The world hates this "complex" as it is called. They blame it for all mental disorders and marriage breakdowns, and seek to destroy it wherever they can. It is made the excuse for all kinds of permissiveness. For too long we have allowed our children to kick and scream on the floor in a tantrum, or slam the door in a fury. We have told ourselves that it is bad to correct them. Just leave them alone, and they will get over it. Consequently they have grown up without a guilt complex, for they were not made to feel responsible for their behaviour. They were just victims of social circumstances. If they yelled for a bar of chocolate, we gave it to them without question, little realising that one day they would scream for sex and get it! We spared the rod and spoiled the child. We now reap the consequences as they have turned against us. It is these children who form the basis of our new permissive society, and it seems as though many of them have been given over to a reprobate mind.

I feel sick to think that the overwhelming permissiveness of our society is such that attempts to rectify matters only produce a violent reaction. It seems as though the dam has burst upon us. In an attempt to relieve the modern generation of its obligation to God and His laws, our educational authorities are throwing away the baby with the bathwater. An era of anarchy or worse lies just around the corner. It is up to us as Christians to take a strong stand, and to witness to His saving grace and power as never before. I was delighted to see on television a few weeks ago a contingent of young people marching through the streets of Bristol as they supported a gospel campaign, waving banners, indicating their Christian stand. One banner captivated me. It read, *FAITH NOT FILTH*. We could do with more of these peaceful demonstrations. Millions of viewers must have seen what I saw. It was a good testimony. May I appeal to all young committed Christians by saying in the words of Scripture, "Keep yourself pure". You can only do this as Christ takes full possession of your life. This is an inheritance of the most inestimable value to yourself and to society, and something which you will cherish to your dying day.

If this proposed film is shown in our schools, then a trail of havoc is sure to follow in its wake. I can think of nothing less desirable than to exhibit such intimacy and vulgarity to hot-blooded young teenagers, with a resulting rampage of indecency, promiscuity and assault. Let us pray that the authorities will be given the courage to restrain such viewings of uninhibited sex, and see that the perpetrators are restricted from further exploitations of this nature. Why should not we as Christian men and women rise up and protest against this wave of permissiveness which is invading our country at this time by vigorously testifying to His wonderful saving grace and power? This is the only answer to a situation which grows more perilous each day.

The author differentiates between the wide range of beautiful and sacred liberties within Christian marriage, demanding absolute faithfulness, and the life of celibacy without, demanding absolute abstinence. God's standards have not changed, and Christ's victory in all areas of sex habits and relationships is assured.

24

Stolen Ropes

*Be sure your sin will find
you out. (Numbers 32:23)*

A friend of mine in Scotland planned an itinerary of meetings for me for a whole month. When I arrived at his home, I found an immaculate filing system with all the necessary correspondence covering my entire stay. He had done a wonderful job. Busy though he was in the involvement of his own commercial travelling which often brought him home after midnight, and up to his neck in Christian activities in his own local church, he had found time to make my representation of Trans World Radio in many parts of Scotland a reality. I found him to be a man of exceptional integrity and he often accompanied me to the meetings, where his help in fixing up the equipment and arranging the bookstall was so much appreciated.

One night we were travelling to a meeting in Dundee and on the way back we bought some fish and chips in Perth. It was delightful to sit in the warm car on that cold evening as we consumed our piping hot supper straight out of the newspaper. Some of us are convinced that it tastes better that way! It was during these times of happy fellowship that he told me a remarkable story which I want to pass on to you. It was something that happened during the course of his business.

Things were not too easy for him at the office, where his Christian honesty was despised by his managing director. The philosophy of this hard man was something like this. It is not really wrong to steal two shillings at times. It may not even be wrong to steal one or two hundred pounds, provided you are not found out... but, of course, if it involves a thousand, that is definitely out. One day our friend discovered some brand new ropes lying in the doorway of the office. They were so good, that he wondered where they might have come from. As he was examining them the manager turned up and asked what he thought of them.

"Fine," was the reply, "but where did you get them?"

"Oh, I gave the B.R.S. transport driver ten shillings to leave them behind!" was the answer.

Naturally our Christian friend was greatly perturbed and, of course, it led to quite a discourse on dishonesty.

"Now what would you say if one of our drivers came back and said he had lost the ropes and you discovered he had been given ten shillings for them?" asked our friend.

"Well, that hasn't happened," was the answer, "and it hasn't got anything to do with this situation. I wouldn't acquire them from just anybody, but British Road Services have plenty of other people's money. You are too honest, that's the trouble with you!"

My friend commented, "No good will come of those ropes, that's for sure!" And there the matter rested.

Shortly afterwards a great truck load of material set out from the store tied with these ropes. As the driver was going along a perfectly straight section of road every rope broke, throwing the heavy, awkward load over the tops of tail, prickly hawthorn hedges, down into a deep gully many feet lower than the level of the road. There was no easy way out. The nearest gate was half a mile away. The driver was frantic! It was difficult enough to recover the load from the gully and to take it to the nearest gate, but still more difficult to reload it from road level. It cost the firm more than half a day's work to sort things out. The ten shillings' gain had resulted in many pounds' loss and the ropes were ruined into the bargain.

As my friend made his way to the scene of the accident, he found a member of the staff carefully examining the broken ropes. The man was scratching his head in sheer amazement. "How could brand new ropes break like this?" he asked. He was a man who had spent years in the business and knew all about the strength of new ropes. Every one of them had snapped without any sign of fraying beforehand.

My friend was ready. "I said no good would ever come of those ropes, Bill," he answered. "They were stolen ropes. The boss gave you ten shillings to get the B.R.S. driver to leave them behind, and this is what has come of it. Believe it or not, an invisible Hand sheared every rope on the top of the load. Is there any other explanation?"

Back at the office an infuriated boss was bemoaning the loss of half a day's work and blaming the driver for the misfortune. My friend turned up. "Don't you realise," he said, "that the load was secured with those stolen ropes? Didn't I tell you that no good would come out of them?" The sullen man had to listen again as my friend tried to reinforce his argument by his Christian testimony.

"Be sure your sin will find you out." This man was learning the hard way. To him there were degrees of honesty according to circumstances. There was no harm in robbing a government concern, when, he said, the government was robbing him in taxes. Therefore, to bribe the driver into leaving the ropes behind was merely to do a good turn to someone in order to get back some of his own money. Surely this could not be dishonest!

What a philosophy! The Bible is absolutely clear when it says, "There is a way which seemeth right unto a man, but the end thereof are the ways of death."

I learned that this dishonest director was a man who never kept his word. His life was completely self-centred, and agreements drawn up were never ratified on paper, but were broken again and again. My friend was seeking the Lord's mind as to whether he should continue with the firm or not. As long as he could witness for his Master he felt there was still an opportunity for this man to find Christ.

It was refreshing to discover someone whose integrity would not readily leave a man in the lurch by a resignation which could jeopardise his business. To me, he was every inch a Christian and when he said to his boss, "No good will ever come of those ropes, that's for sure," he was expressing the mind of God. It was actually a statement of faith. He did not argue about the man's dishonesty, which was an accepted fact. He simply stated that no good would come of those stolen ropes and the Lord vindicated his statement in a wonderful way.

Is there anything dishonest about the way you conduct your business? "Be sure your sin will find you out!" A white lie over the phone to establish some useful connections or to secure a deal cannot bring any good. Jacob's schemes to steal Esau's birthright and blessing forced him from his mother's protective custody for ever and flung him into the arms of his equally cunning Uncle Laban with disastrous results. God meant him to have these things, but not in the way he obtained them. Unless our integrity based on the Word of God is allowed to shape our lives we, too, will be inclined to accept varying degrees of honesty as the normal thing and no good will ever come of it.

We live in a world of sub-standards in almost every sphere of life. Indeed I have heard it openly said that it doesn't really matter if two young people have to get married provided their marriage is a happy one! I repeat my friend's statement to his boss. "No good will ever come out of these ropes, that's for sure." It was an amazing yet perfectly true statement, which could apply to many circumstances in our lives today. "Be sure your sin will find you out."

The answer is, of course, to hand our lives and our circumstances over to the control of the Lord Jesus Christ. Someone has said, "With Christ constantly in control and completely in command, nothing can go wrong." I agree. We may lose out on some business deal which looks most attractive. We may miss an opportunity of securing something for ourselves because our convictions compel us to do so, but nothing but good can come out of any situation which bears the stamp of honesty and integrity in the name of Jesus Christ.

25

The Growth of Weeds

*The care of this world, and the
deceitfulness of riches, choke the
word. (Matthew 13:22)*

My wife and I and our daughter, Ruth, had spent a day in the
garden. It was a glorious day, Whit Monday, and we were at
it for about twelve hours, weeding, hoeing, digging, planting,
sowing and cutting! The consequence was that we could hardly
move. Muscles that had not beep exercised for some time had
been hard at work, and we were so tired at the end of the day
that we could not even sleep at night. At one point I had had
to remove some very long grass that had defied the mower, and
so I had just had to pluck it all up by hand. I felt like Nebu-
chadnezzar and thought of his madness, wondering if I had
the same complaint!

It is not often that I spend bank holidays in this way, as for
years I have been busy ministering God's Word at some house

party or conference. However, since we have been in England we do not get many invitations of this nature, and I wonder if there is the same interest as there used to be. I never was any good at gardening, but a day's hard work certainly reaps its benefit. It is a sheer delight to sit and quietly admire God's handiwork. We certainly live in a delightful locality, surrounded on all sides by flowering shrubs and trees, made all the more attractive by a little elbow grease. We also have some lovely Christian neighbours as well.

As I laboriously removed all kinds of weeds, occasionally having to ask my kind neighbour if I was destroying some plants as well, I thought to myself how readily these unwanted and undesirable elements take root and respond to neglect. They seem to find a lodging place everywhere. Some can easily be pulled out, root and all, but others are much more stubborn and embed themselves deeply, having to be carefully loosened and then dug out with desperation. We found one kind of weed which proved to be a breeding ground for hundreds of aphids, adjacent to the rose beds. Another was a potential source of hay-fever, and was removed without a pang of remorse. I am an inveterate sufferer! The end of the day saw a tremendous pile of garbage fit only for the compost heap or bonfire, but what a difference this made to the appearance of the flower beds and herbaceous borders!

I thought of the Lord and His garden. There are some beautiful and fragrant species of humanity, all so different, and each complementing the other, making a wonderful show for the Heavenly Gardener to enjoy. The infinite variety, even the difference in colouring and exquisite markings, are all there for Him. Their prayers ascend like sweet perfume, and whether they be delightful little buds or mature full-grown blossoms, they all make His heart rejoice. And whether they grow together and multiply into glorious clumps of massed profusion, or find some lonely little spot in which to display their individual glory, they all have a part in His great heart of love.

Yes, the Garden of the Redeemed is a beautiful place. Some of His plants just sit quietly drinking in the sunshine of His love, while the more venturesome climb wildly over any obstacle in their path and delight to overcome the difficulties in their way by smothering the situation with their fragrance in a bold and successful bid for freedom. Others are hardly noticeable until the air is filled with a delightful sense of their perfume. Often the most beautiful are so small that they have to be carefully examined before their exquisite nature is revealed. Some gorgeous varieties flourish in the shade, and it is only after they have terminated their growth that their beauty is seen. Wonderful lessons can be learned from a day in the garden.

But the weeds! Ah, what can we learn from these? It seems they are indeed part of the product of the curse of man's downfall, and readily abound in any uncared for garden. God's people are surrounded by the curse and perhaps now as never before these weeds are making an all-out bid to take over His garden. There is really no need for them to gain the mastery, but for neglect. It is because the children of God have neglected to pray with their families; it is because they have neglected to spend a little time in caring for their spiritual growth, that the weeds have taken over. Some Christian parents are more concerned about the social and educational side of their children than the spiritual, and consequently have neglected the weeds. They grow alongside quite harmlessly until the situation allows them to take over. I heard of one Christian couple who encouraged their daughters in ballet and ballroom dancing. These young ^people are today almost unreachable for Christ because they have been smothered with weeds for years. Some weeds are very attractive, and for a time seem to act as a good cover for neglected areas, until their deep roots strangle everything else out of existence.

It is laborious work tending a garden, so some Christians would prefer to concrete everything in rather than enjoy its benefits. In this way they have encouraged their children to become lazy and indifferent, and the art of weed removal and destruction has become unnecessary. Consequently, the modern generation can no longer differentiate between a beautiful plant and an obnoxious weed. They all look the same outwardly until the weeds take over. To many people, sin is no longer sin until they are found out.

As I grabbed hold of that tough grass, I thought of the weeds of bad habits, so difficult to remove. In my early days we regarded smoking, drinking, gambling, dancing and immorality as the prime curse of the world in which we lived. Maybe we were wrong. We did not go deep enough. As Christians we tended to judge those who were involved in these sins, until certain standards were set up making everything else legitimate. We forgot that the love of riches, and the desire for fame and honour, the scorn of the fallen, the pride of success, were all equally sinful. Consequently we actually encouraged money making. We did everything to promote our children socially and to give them the best education. Their examination results were more important than Bible Class attendance. We pressed them into making decisions, but forgot to make them into disciples. Eventually many of them saw through our shallowness, and violently reacted. Smoking and drinking were too mild, so they literally turned to 'pot.' Gambling and dancing were insipid, so they threw aside all restraint and jitter-bugged their way to freedom. Secret vice was altogether tame, so they openly lived together. We are reaping the consequences of some false standards somewhere along the line, which failed to cope with the true sin problems of our day and generation.

Perhaps this is why some Christians are now lowering their standards in order to come down to the social level set up by their own foolishness, for the weeds of worldliness wrap themselves more readily around Christians who never smoke, drink, dance, or gamble! It is not what we do not do that counts—it is what we do to discourage the propagation of weeds that prevents them taking over! The sins of omission were constantly pointed out by our Lord. What are we actually doing in His name to prevent His garden from being over-run by the weeds of sin and iniquity? Remember, the greatest encouragement for their growth is to do nothing at all! They propagate themselves without any difficulty. It is not smoking, drinking, gambling, dancing and immorality that bother me personally these days. The question is—what am I doing in Christ's name to enlarge His borders? If I am doing nothing, what is preventing me from getting on with the job? If it is not the old fleshly sins, then it is my selfish pig-headedness and lack of concern for the lost. It is my self-centredness that causes the weeds of sin to spread. It is my materialistic outlook, my personal ambitions, my desperate meanness, my fear of sacrifice, my horror of loneliness, my lack of faith, my false conceptions, my pride of ownership, and much, much more, that is behind the rapid growth of so many weeds. What can be more sinful than that? Truly a day in the garden removing weeds has given me much food for thought.

My wife suggests that we use weed-killer, but until I can firmly establish in my mind the difference between weeds and good growth, until I can safely use the killer without fear of destroying anything else, I am a little wary about this. It would certainly save an awful lot of time. Too many Christians have been guilty of using the killer method. It is useless to tell the newly converted that they are not expected to attend the local dance any more, much less to denounce them for it. The weed-killer is too drastic. They will learn, as the Holy Spirit takes them in hand. The gradual systematic method of gently removing the offending weeds cannot be beaten, and you are less likely to damage the surrounding young plants as well.

The bindweed is one of the most fascinating weeds. In its infancy, it is comparatively easy to pull it out of the hedge and uproot it, but when it gets a hold, when it slowly but surely twines itself around the plants until its stranglehold needs a sharp knife to break its grip, then you realise what a menace it is. So it is with sin! When it gains the mastery over our lives, then we begin to realise something of its deadly grip. How wonderful to know that the Heavenly Gardener has provided a remedy. To those who submit to His will and make Christ the Lord of their lives, He gives freedom and liberty from sin. The words of the old hymn writer come to mind; "He breaks the power of cancelled sin and sets the prisoner free..."

There may be weeds in our own spiritual garden, seeking to invade the whole area of our lives, to rob them of blossom and fruit. The only thing to do is to be ruthless with them all. It is no use neglecting the situation, for they will grow without any help from us. We must look for their insidious growth and rid ourselves of their menace without delay. I learned quite a bit about gardening the other day, and I trust it has been a blessing to you as well.

26

Getting Excited

*To be with Christ which is far
better (Philippians 1:23)*

We had planned a motoring trip to Scotland where a number
of meetings had been arranged over Easter in the delightful
city of Inverness. We decided to make the journey in stages,
staying off each night with friends or relatives en route.

The first night was spent in Knutsford with a delightful
young couple who came out to Fiji on a Government contract
when we were serving the Lord in Suva some years ago. Their
two little girls, now teenagers, were born and brought up in
Fiji while we were there, and we shared Christian fellowship for
many years. It was a real joy to meet up with Ruth and David
again, and we had quite a hilarious time looking at pictures
and slides, and recounting memories of old times.

It was then we were told that David's young niece Joy, had
passed away quite suddenly and unexpectedly since our last visit,

when we had accompanied David and Ruth to the Stephen Olford Campaign in Manchester several months before. As a matter of fact they had all been members of the Crusade choir. The story of Joy's passing was so thrilling that we knew at once it would make a wonderful *Gems of Grace* radio talk. It's an up-to-date account of a young woman who was perfectly ready to depart this life to be with her Lord and Saviour.

Joy was a radiant young Christian nurse of twenty-two years of age, serving on the staff of the Withington Hospital in Manchester. She had come to Christ as a child, and had grown up in a Christian home in the Bristol area. She had no close attachments, no particular boy friend, but loved her Lord and Master dearly. Her Christian testimony in the hospital, and her dedicated association with her local church, gave glory to God in a radiant disposition which displayed His grace in a truly amazing way.

A few months ago, Joy was seemingly as well as any young healthy person could have wished to be, but now she has gone to be with her Lord. Apparently she discovered that she was bruising easily, and decided to have a medical check-up to verify the symptoms. The condition was indeed serious, and perhaps you can visualise her reactions when she was told that she only had a month to live. She had picked up a most vicious form of leukaemia and there was no possible hope of recovery. A young girl on the threshold of life, with everything in front of her, had the sentence of death pronounced by the medical authorities with only one month to go.

Some of you listening to me now may react in different ways. Why did she not take the matter to the Lord by faith and claim Divine healing? How can you account for the fact that her Master allowed this thing to happen? Did she not panic at the thought of leaving her parents and loved ones at such a young age? Was there any apprehension of death and what lay beyond the grave?

Yes, all these questions are no doubt going through your mind as I relate this story. They have been through mine too. As I prepare this talk in my study I can hear the birds singing outside. Through the window I can see the delightful green foliage of an awakening Spring. Masses of drooping yellow flowers from a laburnum tree and a profusion of lilac blossom speak of the Great Creator's handiwork. My wife's voice over the phone downstairs assures me of the presence of a loved one who cares for me. Pussy has discovered my whereabouts and rubs my legs as she purrs contentedly. If I knew that in a month's time I would have to leave all this behind me forever, what would my reactions be? Joy's mother seemed almost heartbroken and expressed her feelings in a truly motherly way. She said she would have been prepared to die several times on behalf of her daughter who had seen so little of life down here. Both parents as Christians did not rebel at the thought of losing their only daughter. They were just sad, that's all, sad and mystified to think she would be leaving them so soon. What would your reaction be if this happened to your child?

Well, as Christians, although sad at times, we cannot afford to dwell on the gloomy side, but must look at the bright side as well. If we are rightly related to God through Jesus Christ our Lord... if we know our sins forgiven and we are walking in fellowship with God, there is really nothing to fear about the mystery of death. This last enemy has been finally destroyed by Christ who! died to take away its sting.

We naturally fear the grave and what lies beyond if our' sins have not been forgiven, and of course we tremble at the thought of coming judgment if we are not born again of the Holy Spirit. "It is appointed unto man once to die, and after that the judgment." But when Christ has already removed this judgment when He took the weight of our sin upon Him at Calvary's cross, what is there to fear?

Jesus said to those who repented and turned to Him "In my Father's House are many mansions: if it were not so I would have told you: I go to prepare a place for you." I feel convinced that when we do have to leave this scene with all its delightful associations (and it is a wonderful world when Christ transforms our lives) then what lies ahead must be infinitely more beautiful than we can ever hope to imagine.

To get back to Joy. What was her reaction to the whole situation? What did she have to say about it all? This is really the crux of the whole matter. That is why I spoke with such conviction and delight on Easter Sunday morning to a large congregation at the West Presbyterian Church in Inverness. It was Joy's own testimony that really mattered. It was her own words that counted most. Listen to this...

Shortly after the doctor's verdict had predicted that she would not live for more than a month, Joy was heard to say to a friend "I've only two more weeks to go and I'm getting quite excited." Oh, let me repeat her own testimony once more... "I've only two more weeks to go, and I'm getting quite excited!"

What a thrilling reassurance from a lovely young woman who knew she was right with God through Jesus Christ her Lord. This isn't the testimony of someone with one foot in the grave already... it's a thrilling, vibrating, eternal word of personal assurance, from a radiant personality with the whole of life in front of her, yet someone with all the prospects of an eternal future with her Lord and Master in place of the alluring hopes of life down here below. And in the light of that she was able to say "I'm getting quite excited."

Joy passed away peacefully as predicted with a sudden brain haemmorhage, and she was ushered into the presence of her Lord in this speedy way. The funeral service, conducted by an old friend of mine, Alan Nute, was a triumph of Christ's defeat of sin, death and the grave. An obituary column in the paper aroused the attention of a perfect stranger, a woman who wanted to know all the circumstances of Joy's death. There were several telephone conversations until the woman said "I know about Jesus Christ. It's not as though I don't believe in Him, but how can He contact me? How can I get in touch with Him in the way Joy did? Joy's parents replied "By repenting of your sins and simply receiving Him by faith into your heart. That's all there is to it." The woman thanked them and rang off. When she phoned the next time it was to say that after she had previously replaced the receiver, there and then, in that phone booth, she accepted the Lord into her heart, and was now rejoicing in her salvation. Yes, even in her death, Joy had led another precious soul to Christ.

I wonder if you and I could say what Joy said "I've only got two more weeks to go, and I'm getting quite excited."

27

Under Control

"Thou hast held me by my right hand..." (Psalm 73:23)

Many years ago, as a young schoolboy, I owned a kite. I suppose it's every boy's ambition to fly one of these fascinating things, and mine was no exception. On one occasion I can remember my kite reaching great heights on a beach in Porthcawl in South Wales, as it soared in the direction of the sand-dunes on the banks of the river Ogmore.

If you have ever tried to fly a kite you will realise that in getting it to reach the heights in this way is no small achieve-ment. It was a perfect day and there was enough wind to make kite-flying a real success. However, every boy is impatient to make most of the time when he gets to the sea, and I wanted to join the others in a swim. My kite was flying so beautifully, that I felt it almost a waste of time to draw it back to earth, so I hit on a good plan. I decided to tie it to my father's deck-chair while I was taking the plunge. There would be enough weight to hold it down, as my father was quite a heavy man, and I would retrieve it later.

As I was enjoying the cool swim, I tried in vain to trace my kite in the sky. Oh well, perhaps it had soared to even greater heights and by this time could be out of sight. There were other kites around anyway. I could easily have mistaken mine for somebody else's. After the swim I made my way up the beach to find no father and no kite!

My mother informed me that Dad had gone off to look for it, as somehow it had become detached. Possibly the cord had snapped when my Father had attempted to adjust the deck-chair. My disappointment was acute. We hunted the sand-hills in vain, for my precious kite had plunged to earth or sea never to be seen again. The deck-chair, which had acted as its steadying hand, no longer served its purpose, and without its anchor the kite was useless.

My brother and I often tried to fly a kite with an inadequate tail, and the thing would tear around in circles, or bob up and down erratically, never able to catch the breeze and make a good ascent. We certainly learned the importance of a good stabiliser.

At other times the breeze would be either too gentle or too stiff, no weather for kite flying at all, and the thing would do everything but fly. Yes, the kite must be well designed for flying, have a good tail, and catch the right breeze.

But there is something equally important. If a kite is to soar the heights in a majestic kind of way, it must also have a guiding hand as well. The cord holding it to earth must be strong and light, and the hand holding the cord must be firm. The very success of the kite's soaring ability is in the hand that controls it. When out of control, the kite is useless and plunges to its destruction immediately. What a lesson for us to learn today.

The famous preacher, John Newton, composed a poem which emphasises the truth of man's wilfulness and God's over-ruling providence. His poem was about a kite...

> *"Once upon a time a paper kite, mounted to a wondrous height,*
> *Where giddy with its elevation, it thus expressed self-admiration,*
> *'See how the crowds of gazing people, admire my flight above the steeple,*
> *How they would wonder if they knew, all that a kite like me can do.*
> *Were I but free, I'd take a flight and pierce the clouds beyond their sight,*
> *But ah, like a poor prisoner bound, my string confines me to the ground.*
> *I'd brave the eagles towering wing, might I but fly without the string'*
> *It tugged and pulled while thus it spoke... to snap the string, at last it broke,*
> *Deprived at once of all its stay, in vain it tried to soar away,*
> *Unable its own weight to bear, it fluttered downward through the air...*
> *'Ah, foolish kite, thou hast no wing,*
> *HOW COULDS'T THOU FLY WITHOUT THE STRING?'*
> *My heart cried out, O Lord, I see, how much this kite resembles me,*
> *Forgetful that by Thee I stand, impatient of Thy ruling hand,*
> *How oft I've wished to break the lines, Thy wisdom for my lot assigns,*

How oft indulge the vain desire, for something more, or
*   something higher,*
But for Thy grace and love divine, a fall this dreadful
*   had been mine...*

To lose the guidance of God's right hand and the cord
of His restraint, would be to fall into immediate sin and
destruction. We would be like a kite without its cord, plunging crazily to our doom instead of exploring the heights of
spiritual achievement. The very gravitational pull of the world,
acting against the uplifting forces of God's Holy Spirit, enables
us to overcome as Jesus takes control. Yes, "the law of the
spirit of life in Christ Jesus has made me free from the law
of sin and death." As long as God's guiding hand is upon
our lives, the downward forces of evil are counteracted by
the upward surge of His mighty power, and we overcome in
Jesus' Name. In other words, God uses the very forces of evil
to help the Christian in his daily walk and warfare! There is
nothing frightening about temptation to those who come
under God's control as this is the very means of living victori-
ously in Christ's Name! Without these forces of evil we would
become flabby and spineless. The pull of the world, the flesh,
and the devil are all necessary for us to reach spiritual heights
of great nobility, provided God holds the string. It is simply
wonderful to contemplate these thoughts expressed in such a
simple thing as boy's kite.

As I look back over the years and visualise my kite soaring
in the breeze on that lovely summer day, I can still recognise
its dangerous situation hundreds of feet above the earth, but
as long as a firm hand held the cord there could be no pend-
ing disaster. We shall never be free from danger, but there
will never be disaster. A life gripped by God's right hand is
absolutely under control, however dangerous the situation,

and disastrous consequences are avoided. To be free from His restraint is to sever the very cords of His love and protection. Is His hand upon your life and mine today?

There is a tremendous cry for freedom in the modem world, and it is extremely difficult to tell others that only a life of restraint, a life under God's holy restraint, is free to breath the fragrant atmosphere of joy and liberty. Men and women around us in attempting to throw aside all human restraint to find freedom, have found .themselves plunging out of control like a kite without a guiding hand. Their so-called liberty has turned to license, and their desire to disaster. Like kites out of control they fly around in circles, careering erratically from place to place, until at last they plunge headlong to destruction. Yes, we can learn many wonderful lessons from such a simple thing as a kite. When the Lord holds the cord, the gravitational pull of those evil forces around us assist in keeping us spiritually airborne, "raised with Him in newness of life," resulting in perfect freedom and liberty. That's just what Jesus said... "If the Son shall make you free, you shall be free indeed..."

28

Kufstein Glass

"As clay in the Potter's Hand..."
(Jeremiah 18:6)

One of the highlights of our trip to Austria was a visit to the glass-works at Kufstein, and we were fascinated to see how the fine glass goblets and tumblers are made. Before a beautiful work of art in glass can be produced, all its impurities have to be burned out in the furnace. We watched this being done, and saw the surplus molten glass removed in thick shapeless masses of red hot material on the end of a blowpipe which constantly revolved in the hands of a skilled expert. Who would ever imagine that those remaining big blobs of ugly molten clay could be transformed into the most exquisite clearcut crystal glasses? It is not sufficient for us to know our sins forgiven, although this is wonderful news indeed. The forgiven sinner becomes, in God's hands, valuable material for shaping to His own ends, but until we have passed through the fires of affliction we are not going to be worth much to Him, are we? You see, Christ forgives our sins, then He has to get to work to deliver us from the impurities of sin before we can be used to glorify God in our daily lives. This is something like the fusion of silica and sand in the furnace. The only material God can use is the clay of our redeemed humanity and then He takes all the gritty substance and through the fires of affliction begins to burn out the dross and makes us pliable in His hands as red hot candidates of the cross. The process is painful but essential. Impurities must go if my life is to become a vessel of honour, worthy of His great Name. Then when I am still white hot in His hands, He can mould me to shape. We saw one piece of glass rejected because it cooled off too quickly and became brittle. The workman just broke it to pieces and rejected it, possibly throwing it into the melting pot again... reminding us of what happens to luke-warm Christians.

I thought of my life, potentially useless, until melted and moulded by my Maker, and with fascination watched the transformation take place as the skilled workmen puffed a little air down the long tube to which was attached a blob of molten glass. Instantly it began to take shape, and now appeared as a big bubble. Not for one moment did the blowers allow the liquid glass to remain still. It was moving all the time, revolving in the air as it gradually cooled off and took its new shape. So it is with the wind of God's Spirit. When we are being moulded to God's requirements, no longer resisting His will, the Holy Spirit begins to fill us. We then take shape. Yes, we saw the gradual transformation take place before our very eyes. Instruments were used to contour the material before it cooled off, just as a potter uses his hands on the clay, and it wasn't long before we saw a beautifully shaped goblet emerge from the process. Once more it had to pass through a second heating process on moving bands in an oven which gradually decreased in temperature until it appeared without a crack or a flaw as an object of worth at the other end. Note that gentle puffs of air first patterned the glass. When the Spirit of God gently blows upon our consecrated lives, we, too, will emerge from the trial or testing as an object of worth to God. Christ's death for us makes us available to God and determines our destination, whereas our death with Christ makes our availability worth while to God and determines our destiny.

There is yet even another job of work which makes the whole process much more valuable, for the cutters have yet to get to work on it. That beautifully shaped piece of glass, now useful for drinking purposes, must catch the light and reflect its Maker's design so that it becomes not only useful but attractive. It is of no real value to anybody until the cutter weaves his design into it and it bears his image. We watched the experts at their benches, cutting the most exquisite patterns into the glass on their lathes. We noted that a jet of water cooled the instruments, so that the glass would not crack or break under the strain. The Lord never allows His servants to be tempted above they are able to bear, and the lesson is obvious. Not only does the fire of affliction make us pliable in His hands but this is often followed by adversity, persecution and testing, which leave their mark in the most exquisite way. The deeper the cut, the more valuable the design. Some objects were almost priceless. Crystal vases, bowls and jugs were on display and we marvelled at the intricate patterns which were skilfully and delicately traced by the cutter's sharp knife. So it is with the child of God who submits to His Maker and Redeemer. If there is any undue resistance, the object of intended beauty is shattered and rejected. It is only when we yield to the pressure of God's Holy Spirit that we become transformed from a worthless bit of human clay into a vessel fit for the Master's use.

There was yet something else which fascinated us. Beautiful crystal catches the light and reflects its image. In addition to the natural element, some designers had incorporated the deepest colourings into their glassware to add to the already attractive decoration. We saw the most exquisite reds, blues, and greens, in graduating tones, highlighting the quality of their productions and causing the crystal to scintillate like flashing gems. The Christian not only reflects the image of God, Who is Light, but he also radiates something of the glory of the cross of Christ, and in effect he becomes a colourful being. There is nothing drab about discipleship. Woven into the intrinsic design of redemption is the deep scarlet of His precious blood, the heavenly blue of His humanity and the evergreen of His eternity. When our Lord said in effect "Let your light so shine..." He had in mind an object of intense beauty reflecting the glory of God—your life and mine in His Hands. My eyes caught sight of a crystal jug into which a delightful shade of pinks and reds had been blended, and because it was not too expensive I decided to purchase it for my wife. We had to turn a blind eye to a set of matching glasses, but now the jug is an object of beauty and usefulness on our sideboard, a reminder of our trip to the glassworks at Kufstein in Austria.

Oh, there is something else I had almost forgotten. My wife always likes to test crystal by clipping the rim of the object with her fingers. If there is nothing but a dead response, then it is not genuine. Much that looks like the real thing is a cheap article that is mass-produced and never responds with a clear cut ring. Good crystal always resonates. It must ring true. How like your Christian life and mine! Paul spoke of being like a clanging symbol instead of a musical vibration. When our lives take shape as being of some worth to God, then we shall sing praises to the One Who has delivered us so mightily. There will be a note of victory, a song of praise, and a vibrant response of heart. The wind of the Spirit, the work of the Master and the cutting edge of the Maker will produce an article that rings true. There will be no spurious imitation, for the stamp of Divine ownership declares the genuine product. The cross in human experience will bear witness to the fact that we belong to the Lord.

Remember, if you are to be of worth to God, your life must go into the furnace of affliction for all the dross to be removed. There is no other way, and if the furnace is hot beloved, remember what happened to the glass at Kufstein. Then the cutting process follows. Something may be cutting deeply into your life today, but the Divine workman is an expert. He knows what He is doing. As the sharp edge gets to work it is cooled by the water of His Word. This "washing" is essential. Soak in it, and the outcome will be a vessel meet for the Master's use. Having melted us and moulded us He wants to fashion us and use us. Then when the article is complete He delights to fill it with Himself. Oh may that be our experience—an empty vessel, shaped to His own Divine requirements, and filled to overflowing with the Spirit of God!

Our visit to Kufstein taught us many valuable lessons, reminding us of that delightful refrain...

"Something beautiful, something good.
All my confusion He understood,
All I had to offer Him was brokenness and strife,
But He made something beautiful of my life!"

Bob and Cynthia Stokes

Walking Together Press is a non-profit publishing company devoted to supporting grassroots libraries in Africa through global book sales and through providing free library editions.

To read our story, to see our catalog, and to learn more about how you can help us in our mission, visit our website at:

https://walkingtogether.press